Contents

Summary

Every Child Matters is a comprehensive programme of reform for children's services. Key underpinning principles—all garnering very broad support in the evidence we have received—include: more closely integrated frontline delivery of educational, health, social and specialist services; earlier intervention to provide support before problems become serious; closer working between professionals who might be involved with the same child or young person; more coherent planning and commissioning of services at the combined local level—and the establishment of Children's Trusts (or similar arrangements) to support this; and greater involvement of children, parents and carers in the development of services.

More generally, the drive to improving both universal and targeted services in the same suite of reforms has been very well received. It is supported by research evidence which demonstrates the value of early intervention to prevent serious problems developing, coupled with targeted and specialist support where necessary. The Government needs to be commended at the outset for embarking on such an ambitious and wide-ranging programme of root-and-branch reform.

We have been impressed by the commitment, dedication and enthusiasm demonstrated by those responsible for delivering the reforms at the front line. There is considerable evidence of progress already been made on the development of integrated, user-centred services in some areas. Other areas have much further to go and ensuring consistency across the country is likely to be challenging in the extreme—implementation will be the litmus test for *Every Child Matters*, and the Government needs to remain attentive to the kinds of support and direction that local areas need.

Some specific aspects of the reforms give us cause for concern. The Government has proposed the establishment of a network of computerised 'child indexes' (or databases) containing basic details on all children in England, to aid communication between professionals. These proposals are not currently well-grounded in research evidence. Crucial decisions to go ahead in principle were taken before it could be demonstrated that the indexes would be worthwhile and that practical problems with security and keeping information up to date could be overcome. We welcome the reassurances given to us by the Minister for Children, Young People and Families that she would proceed slowly and would not enter into commissioning arrangements for child indexes lightly, and that more research will be undertaken before going ahead.

Some extra resources are being made available for implementation of *Every Child Matters*, but the Government has repeatedly said that it expects improvements to services to be largely resourced from mainstream non-ring-fenced budgets and savings derived from more integrated and coherent services. Witnesses have told us that this will be difficult to achieve in practice. Workforce development for in-service staff is of critical importance, but it is likely to be resource intensive. It is not clear that services will be able to meet the costs that this will incur. The initial set-up of Children's Trust arrangements is also likely to be costly, yet minimal funding is being provided directly for this purpose. The Government therefore needs to lead from the top and provide evidence of how efficiency savings and improved services might be achieved concurrently.

Some crucial services—such as schools and General Practitioners—have not been placed under a direct 'duty to co-operate' in local Children's Trust partnership arrangements. The Government argues that these agencies will be encouraged to participate by levers in the system such as inspection and through their relationships with Local Authorities and Primary Care Trusts respectively. However, we do not think that these levers are likely to be powerful enough. There is a real risk that a minority of schools and GPs could choose not to participate, fundamentally undermining the ethos of *Every Child Matters*.

Every Child Matters, although based in the Department for Education and Skills, requires co-ordination and joined-up working with other Government departments—especially the Department of Health and the Home Office. While sincere efforts are being made to promote joined-up working, there are still some tensions between different policies affecting children and young people emanating from different departments. In particular, the Youth Justice system and the immigration system currently operate in ways which can be seen to undermine the aims of *Every Child Matters*. These tensions need to be tackled at Ministerial level if the Government is to convince us that every child really does matter equally.

1 Introduction

1. In 2003, the Government launched *Every Child Matters,* a comprehensive programme of reform for children's services with wide-reaching implications for education, health, social services, voluntary and community organisations, and other agencies. This was also accompanied by a substantial relocation of existing children's social care policy work (and associated funding) from the Department of Health into the Department for Education and Skills. We therefore thought it timely to conduct an initial overview inquiry of developments in this area, in line with our remit to scrutinise all aspects of departmental policy.

2. The Committee announced its inquiry into *Every Child Matters* on 21 September 2004, with the following terms of reference: To undertake a concise overview of the reforms being proposed for children's services under the banner *Every Child Matters*, focusing particularly on issues that were likely to arise during implementation. We have aimed to gain an understanding of the broad issues of organisational and professional integration, information management and the needs of parents and children, exploring specifically:

- The place of health, social services and education respectively within integrated services;

- The practical implications of the 'duty to collaborate', including funding streams and location of staff and facilities;

- Staff and management needs: team-building, leadership and training;

- Inspection;

- Listening to children; the role of the Children's Commissioner;

- Working with parents;

- The creation, management and sharing of records, including electronic databases.

3. During the course of the inquiry we took evidence from the Rt. Hon Margaret Hodge, Minister for Children, Young People and Families; Lord Laming of Tewin; Philip Collins, Director, Social Market Foundation; Ofsted; Commission for Social Care Inspection; Healthcare Commission; Audit Commission; Local Government Association; Association of Directors of Social Services; Association of Directors of Education and Children's Services; Confederation of Education Service Managers; NHS Confederation; Association of Chief Police Officers; Children's Rights Alliance for England; National Society for the Prevention of Cruelty to Children; Professor Kathleen Marshall, Commissioner for Children and Young People in Scotland; Peter Clarke, Commissioner for Children in Wales; Nigel Williams, Commissioner for Children and Young People for Northern Ireland; Family Policy Alliance; Dr Deborah Ghate, Director, Policy Research Bureau; Professor Hedy Cleaver, Royal Holloway College, University of London; Dr Eileen Munro, London School of Economics; Richard Thomas, Her Majesty's Information Commissioner; Department for Education and Skills and the Department of Health. We received over 70 written memoranda, which have aided us in our work.

4. We are grateful to our specialist advisers, Professor Bob Hudson, Professor Chris Pascal, Dr Rosemary Peacocke, Teresa Smith and Professor Kathy Sylva, for their assistance with this inquiry.

2 Background

Lord Laming's inquiry into the death of Victoria Climbié

5. Eight-year old Victoria Climbié died from hypothermia on 25 February 2000 after months of sustained abuse at the hands of her foster-carer and Great Aunt, Marie-Therese Kouao and her partner Carl John Manning. Following Victoria's death, the Home Office and the Department of Health invited Lord Laming of Tewin to chair an independent statutory review of the circumstances surrounding her murder and to make recommendations to prevent, as far as possible, similar cases arising in the future. The report of the inquiry team was published in January 2003, and makes over a hundred recommendations for action[1].

6. Lord Laming's report concluded that Victoria's death had been entirely preventable—12 key occasions were identified where services could have successfully intervened to prevent Victoria coming to further harm. In each case the opportunity was missed. The inquiry team identified systemic problems which had militated against successful intervention. These included: Low standards of professional practice; an absence of a person or persons with accountability; poor managerial support for front line workers; and failure to share information within and between agencies.

Every Child Matters—key proposals

7. *Every Child Matters*[2] constituted the Government's policy response to the findings and recommendations of Lord Laming's Inquiry. It was published as a Green Paper for consultation on 8 September 2003, concurrently with the Government's recommendation-by-recommendation response to Lord Laming's report..[3]

8. Consultation on the original Green Paper indicated broad support for its aims and objectives. Its proposals have since been further developed in subsequent documents including *Every Child Matters; Next Steps*[4] and *Every Child Matters; Change for Children*[5]. At the time of our inquiry, additional guidance on specific aspects of the reforms was also being published. In tandem, the Department of Health has prepared the *National Service Framework for Children, Young People and Maternity Services*,[6] which sets standards for children's health and social services, and the interface of those services with education.

---

1   *The Victoria Climbié inquiry : Report of an inquiry by Lord Laming*,
        http://www.victoria-Climbié-inquiry.org.uk/finreport/finreport.htm

2   Department for Education and Skills, *Every Child Matters*, CM 5860, September 2003.

3   Department of Health, Department for Education and Skills, and Home Office (2003) *Keeping Children Safe. The Government's Response to the Victoria Climbie Inquiry Report and Joint Chief Inspectors' Report Safeguarding Children*, CM 5861, September 2003.
        http://www.everychildmatters.co.uk/_content/documents/KeepingChildrenSafe.pdf

4   Department for Education and Skills, *Every Child Matters: Next Steps*, DfES/0240/2004, March 2004.
        http://www.everychildmatters.co.uk/_content/documents/EveryChildMattersNextSteps.pdf

5   Department for Education and Skills, *Every Child Matters: Change for Children*, DfES/1110/2004, November 2004
        http://www.everychildmatters.co.uk/_content/documents/Every%20Child%20Matinserts.pdf

6   Department of Health, *National Service Framework for Children, Young People and Maternity Services*, 2004.
        http://www.dh.gov.uk/assetRoot/04/09/05/52/04090552.pdf

9. The Government has been keen to stress that *Every Child Matters* aims to provide more than just a response to the Laming inquiry and has a remit wider than acute services and child protection. Instead, it aims to address the latter in a broader context of earlier intervention and the roll-out of better preventative services. Therefore, existing early intervention and support programmes such as Sure Start, Early Excellence Centres, Children's Centres and extended schools now fall under the *Every Child Matters* banner.

10. *Every Child Matters* aims to bring about root-and-branch reform of children's services at every level to ensure that children and young people achieve five main outcomes. They should:

> - Be healthy
>
> - Stay safe
>
> - Enjoy and Achieve
>
> - Make a positive contribution
>
> - Achieve economic wellbeing

11. The following measures are proposed to bring about 'whole system change':

- Service planning and delivery to be focused on the five outcomes outlined in paragraph 10, above; children, young people, parents and carers to become more closely involved in the design, delivery and management of services.

- More integrated delivery at the front line: multi-disciplinary teams of professionals—including those from health, education and social services—co-located where appropriate in children's centres or Extended Schools.

- More integrated processes available across children's services, including protocols for the sharing of information about individual children; a computerised 'child index' containing basic data about all children; common assessment and referral procedures for identifying and addressing need; joint training with common core standards.

- Local authorities will lead the development of Children's Trusts – these will involve key agencies in the co-ordinated planning, commissioning, funding and delivery of services suited to local needs and priorities.

- Integrated inspections, with Ofsted as the lead agency, will assess how well services work together to improve outcomes for children in local areas.

- Directors of Children's Services and Lead (council) Members will be appointed to take strategic leadership and to be accountable for outcomes for children in their area.

- Integrated governance arrangements to cut across agencies that constitute Children's Trusts.

- Formerly voluntary Area Child Protection Committees will now be replaced by statutory Local Safeguarding Children Boards.

- Governmental responsibilities for many services for children and young people co-located in the DfES under the leadership of a new Minister for Children, Young People and Families.

The Children Act 2004

12. Many of the reforms proposed in *Every Child Matters*—including the establishment of a Children's Commissioner for England—required amendments to statute. Consequently, a Children Bill was presented to Parliament in March 2004 and subsequently received royal assent on 15 November 2004. The Children Act 2004, as it now is, provides the legal 'backbone' for the programme of reform.

13. During the passage of the Act through Parliament, debate focused on a number of particularly contentious issues, including: the role and remit of the Children's Commissioner for England; agencies to be included in the 'statutory duty to co-operate' at local level; the 'reasonable chastisement' justification for capital punishment and amendments to the law on private fostering. These debates continue to resonate with those who have submitted evidence to our inquiry. While it would not be productive to rehearse the debates surrounding the Children Act 2004 in full here, we do refer to them where appropriate.

Initial impressions

14. One very clear message emerges from the evidence we have received: there is almost universal support for the basic aims of *Every Child Matters*. We agree with witnesses—and therefore think it fitting to state at the outset—that the Government deserves substantial praise for embarking on such an ambitious and comprehensive programme of reform.

15. We have been impressed by the commitment and enthusiasm shown by those at the front line, who will shoulder most of the responsibility for implementing the radical and substantial changes in practice. We welcomed the evidence they gave us of the significant progress made to date. However, we also pressed them on their concerns, in practical terms, about how *Every Child Matters* will be translated into reality.

16. Early on in the inquiry, Lord Laming foreshadowed the contribution of many of the witnesses we would subsequently hear from when he told us:

> "I see the steps that the Government has taken, which are very, very important steps and a solid foundation on which to build the beginning of the next phase; however, the test is: what is the quality of services delivered at the front door by any one of these agencies across the whole of England, whether on a housing estate in Preston or a rural community in Cornwall? [...] Implementation will be the test, and what

the Government now puts in place gives us encouragement, but there is a long way to go."[7]

17. While generally welcomed, some aspects of the proposed reforms have been the subject of significant concern and debate. These include: proposals to improve information-recording and sharing through the introduction of a series of linked databases containing basic information on all children in England; the role of the Children's Commissioner for England; and the likely participation of some schools, GPs and health services in the programme of reform. Consequently, we comment on these issues in detail in the relevant parts of this report. Structurally, we follow the DfES's lead, looking first at the central 'outcomes' and then at the implications of change at the front line, process level, strategic level and governance level, in turn.

3 Overarching issues

Pacing change at policy level

18. The Minister for Children has repeatedly stated that *Every Child Matters* should be considered as a programme of transformational rather than gradual or incremental change. Accordingly, policy development has taken place at a formidable speed and has been accompanied by a slew of consultation documents and guidance. This pressure to move so quickly poses some inherent difficulties for a department which has publicly committed itself to implementing evidence-based policy and which is significantly reducing its workforce.

19. A clear example of this tension exists in relation to the development of child indexes or databases. The Government has made a policy commitment to the eventual implementation of computerised records containing basic details about every child in the country, as an aid to communication between staff in different agencies. To assist in the development of best practice, ten local 'Trailblazer' areas were invited to develop and test information sharing and assessment procedures (including computerised child indexes). We have some concerns about whether the policy decision to implement these indexes can truly be said to have followed from a thorough evaluation of Trailblazers' experiences. We have similar concerns about the 35 Pathfinder Children's Trusts, which were set up to trial the new local planning, commissioning and delivery arrangements. The Pathfinders themselves are still at a relatively early stage of development and analysis of their experience is consequently still in progress. Independent evaluation is not due to be completed until 2007, yet most local areas will be expected to have Children's Trust arrangements in place by 2006.[8]

20. **We understand the drive toward rapid transformational change at policy level and think that this is entirely legitimate given the urgency of protecting children better and promoting their development and well-being. However, a Government committed (rightly) to pursuing evidence-based policy has a difficult balance to strike. It is crucial that significant changes are thoroughly trialled and evaluated before roll-out, especially in cases where doing things badly risks worsening outcomes for vulnerable children and young people.**

Local determination and the role of central Government

21. Early on in the development of *Every Child Matters*, the Government was criticised for appearing to favour an overly prescriptive approach, giving local areas little control over the pace and nature of change. There has since been a perceptible policy shift toward local self-determination in response to this criticism and the current position is clearly expressed in the recent implementation plan, *Every Child Matters: Change for Children:*

> "Since the publication of Every Child Matters, we have talked with our partners about how to manage change most effectively, recognising that local leadership,

---

8 The University of East Anglia in association with the National Children's Bureau, have been commissioned to carry out a formal evaluation of Pathfinder Children's Trusts. This will run until 2007. A Phase 1 interim report was published in October 2004 (*National Evaluation of Children's Trusts. Phase 1 interim report.*)

dynamism and ownership are vital if change is to succeed. And there is an important balance to strike between national expectations and local discretion."[9]

22. This move toward local determination has been largely welcomed in the evidence we have seen and heard. We concur that the best outcomes will be achieved if solutions are adapted to local circumstances. However, we also contend that in some areas, more central direction is necessary. For example, some feel that the vision of integrated front line services is currently vague and that there is a need for clear direction and guidance of what integrated front line services should look like in the future. These issues are discussed in more detail in the appropriate sections of the report.

23. **The balance between local determination and action from the centre is likely to remain a critical issue as *Every Child Matters* unfolds. Too much central direction risks alienating those on the ground who know a great deal about local circumstances; too little, on the other hand, risks inconsistency and the appearance of gaps in services. In respect of certain aspects of the reforms, our evidence suggests that more central responsibility and direction may be needed than is currently the case.**

Maintaining political momentum for a ten-year programme of change

24. The Minister for Children has repeatedly stated that *Every Child Matters* will be a long-term programme of reform, with full implementation likely to take at least 10 years. For implementation to be successful there needs to be a sustained commitment at the highest levels of Government throughout this period to drive through change.

25. Our visit to British Columbia gave us food for thought on this issue; there, a similarly ambitious programme of reform for children's services had been only partially successfully implemented. We were told that one of the determining factors had been 'ministerial churn', and that privately, it was felt that a lack of sustained political support over the longer term had been partly responsible for the achievement of only limited success.

26. It would be unnecessarily gloomy to predict that the same fate will befall England's reforms. The Minister for Children told us that she was deeply committed to *Every Child Matters*, and it was reassuring to hear from her that she considered the role 'the best job in Government.'[10] However, we are forced to confront the reality that 'ministerial churn' is likely to occur here, too. The effect of this churn on the ability to provide the vital central leadership for *Every Child Matters* is difficult to predict, but this is something that will need to be monitored over the coming period.

---

9   ibid, p 6.

10   Q 479

4 Placing children, young people and families at the centre of the reforms

An outcomes-based approach

27. *Every Child Matters* aims to put children and young people at the heart of the reforms and has consequently been designed around five 'outcomes' that all children and young people should be able to expect: being healthy; staying safe; enjoying and achieving; making a positive contribution; and achieving economic well-being. These outcomes have been arrived at in consultation with children and young people, and it is intended that they will drive all aspects of children's services reform. We have found almost universal enthusiasm for the outcomes-focused and child-centred approach, of which the following comment from the Children's Society is typical:

> "We [...] greatly welcome and support the key themes of the Green Paper [...] [including] That all policy- and decision-making, funding, commissioning and professional practice should be coherently focussed on a common set of outcomes to be achieved for all children and young people."[11]

28. The pursuit of an outcomes-based approach is clearly only worthwhile if the definitions of each outcome are meaningful and comprehensive. Since the publication of the original Green Paper, the five main outcomes have each been refined to have five associated 'aims' (see Appendix A). We are pleased that the Government has recently consulted on the appropriateness of these 25 aims[12], and look forward to learning the outcome.

29. An outcomes-led approach is also only likely to be meaningful if attainment of the five outcomes—and services' contributions to those outcomes—can be accurately measured. Joint inspections of children's services and individual institutional inspections will be one of the main means for achieving this. How effectively joint inspection in particular *will* assess local progress toward meeting the five outcomes is yet to be determined. Ofsted and partners have recently produced proposals for children's services inspection, on which they are consulting. Our initial thoughts on the new children's services inspections, including their likely effectiveness as a tool for measuring progress towards the five outcomes, are laid out in more detail in section six of this report.

Involving children, young people and parents

30. One key aim of *Every Child Matters* is for children and young people to become more centrally involved in the design and delivery of services that they access, as well as the inspection and evaluation of services. In addition, part two of the Children Act 2004 contains a subsection relating specifically to parents, which stipulates that children's services authorities "must have regard to the importance of parents and other persons caring for children in improving the well-being of children."[13] The underlying

---

11 EVCM 44, para 2.2

12 As part of the consultation on the Integrated Inspection of Children's Services, led by Ofsted.

13 Children Act 2004, Part 2:10 (3).

presumption is that service user involvement will achieve better outcomes for children and their families. It is mostly left to local Children's Trusts to decide the exact means and methods by which these groups will be involved in the design and delivery of services, although we understand that guidance is forthcoming from the DfES on this issue.

31. There is evidence of strong agreement with the value of such an approach. With regard to the involvement of parents and carers, the Family Policy Alliance stressed that their own research had found that effective service delivery was underpinned by six crucial factors, most of which implied a close working relationship with parents and families. These were: reachable services, recognition of the family's need, responses to the need of the whole family, respect for family expertise, referral to services which meet their express need, and checking to see whether support provided was useful[14].

32. The Association of Directors of Social Services similarly emphasised the importance of user involvement—but also stressed that this would be challenging to achieve in practice:

> "there is a set of issues about how we develop a real consistent community voice into children's services. This will fail unless we are engaging children, their families and their communities; and we need to find ways which consistently and imaginatively are going to make people feel they are party to this agenda, and that it is not just an agenda that is being developed by the macro organisations."[15]

33. Philip Collins, Director of the Social Market Foundation, told us that, in his view, it would be those who would most benefit from involvement that would be the most difficult to engage. While there were successful examples of initiatives involving diverse groups in the shaping of services, these were generally resource-intensive:

> "Across all public services it has proved to be quite easy to get some social groups involved in public services and much more difficult for the lower socio-economic groups [but] … Sure Start did it and they did it by going out and knocking on doors essentially. Outreach work was the answer. They got people involved which all the evidence and all the doom sayers said you could not do. The positive answer is that it can be done, but it is expensive because you cannot sit and wait for the people to come. You have to go to them. It is very labour intensive. I do not think at the moment that hard pressed workers in the system have the capacity to do it."[16]

34. An interview with a Pathfinder Children's Trust revealed the following interesting observation on the impact of differential funding and ability to engage users:

> "When we set up the Children's Trust, we were impressed by the Sure Start model of Governance with its emphasis on community ownership. We adapted elements of that model for the Children's Trust. However, Sure Start comes with resources with which to facilitate and promote involvement; the Children's Trust does not."[17]

---

14   EVCM 52, sect. 5.

15   Q 166

16   Q 68

17   University of East Anglia in association with the National Children's Bureau, *National Evaluation of Children's Trusts. Phase 1 interim report*, p 104, Oct 2004.

35. There is a large body of research into effective practical strategies for the involvement of parents and carers in service delivery.[18] Additionally, Sure Start programmes have been at the forefront of promoting parental involvement, and analyses of these programmes that are currently being released provide a useful source of information[19]. Similarly, the independent evaluation of Pathfinder Children's Trusts, being carried out currently by the University of East Anglia,[20] has the potential to inform the development of the guidance mentioned above, and future best practice materials. There is a smaller body of research into successful strategies for involving children and young people in the design and delivery of services, and additional research could be commissioned to strengthen knowledge in this area, especially in the light of the interim review of Pathfinder Children's Trusts, which suggested that involving children and young people has sometimes been more difficult than involving their parents or carers.[21]

36. The issue of parental (and wider community) involvement has recently been thrown into particularly sharp focus by announcements that the funding and governance arrangements for Sure Start programmes are to change. Sure Start programmes currently receive direct funding from the Sure Start Unit, and parents along with community representatives have routinely held places on the board of directors and/or been closely involved in the programmes in other ways. The National Evaluation of Sure Start (NESS) shows this has been popular and empowering for parents, and that Sure Start staff have found parents and carers valuable allies in enhancing service delivery.[22]

37. In the future, funding for Sure Start Children's Centres will be channelled through children's services authorities—who may then involve parents in the operation of centres. Some have interpreted this as representing an implied diminution in the role of parents, and have questioned how this sits with the policy commitment to make sure parents and carers are centrally involved in service design and delivery.

38. The Minister told us that this was categorically not the case and that the intention was to:

> "ensure, both through guidance that we give local authorities and the way in which we inspect and manage the performance of local authorities, that that essential ethos of Sure Start, which is the involvement of parents in all aspects of the delivery of services for children and families in the earliest years, is maintained."[23]

39. These were welcome words, but it remains to be seen whether the effects of a substantial reorganisation of Sure Start will be as intended—and whether parents will continue to have the kinds of roles that they have held until now. **We are concerned that significant changes are being made to the Sure Start programme when evidence about the effectiveness of the current system is only just beginning to emerge. This relates**

---

18 See for example, Moran, Ghate and Van de Merwe, *What works in parenting support?: a review of the international evidence*, 2004 This research review was commissioned by the Department for Education and Skills.

19 See for example National Evaluation of Sure Start, *Implementing Sure Start Local Programmes: An in-Depth Study*, 2005

20 ibid

21 ibid

22 ibid

23 Q 582

back to our wider point[24] about the inherent difficulties of pursuing transformative and rapid change while at the same time maintaining a commitment to evidence-based policy.

Children's Commissioner for England

40. A key proposal in creating a keener focus on the needs of children and young people is the Children's Commissioner for England. Part one of the Children Act 2004 provides for the establishment of a Children's Commissioner for England – the first in the country's history—in direct response to Lord Laming's recommendation that a Children's Commissioner should be appointed. The appointment of Professor Al Ainsley-Green, formerly National Clinical Director for Children at the Department of Health, to the post was announced on 8 March 2005. We wish him well in his endeavours. It is intended that the Children's Commissioner will be a powerful 'listening post' for children and young people, and an important part of the commitment to place children at the centre of reforms. Specific powers to be exercised by the post-holder are broadly defined on the face of the Act and are subject to regulation through guidance to be issued at a later date by the Secretary of State.

41. The overwhelming majority of evidence we have received has welcomed in principle the establishment through statute of a Children's Commissioner for England. However, the scope and powers of the role have attracted very significant criticism. There is concern about: a perceived lack of independence of the Commissioner; lack of clarity about the relationship of the Commissioner for England with the three existing Children's and Young People's Commissioners in the rest of the UK; and the definition of the role as one concerned with promoting the needs and views of children and young people, rather than safeguarding and protecting their rights.

International comparisons

42. England is the last part of the UK to create the role of a Children's Commissioner—similar posts have already been established in the devolved administrations: in Wales Peter Clarke was appointed to the role in 2001; in Northern Ireland, Nigel Williams was appointed in 2003; and in Scotland Professor Kathleen Marshall took up office in 2004. The powers, roles and remits differ slightly between the three existing Children's and Young People's Commissioners. However, the three Commissioners told us that differences between their remits and the remit of the Commissioner for England were more significant—a memorandum from the Commissioners, printed with this report, compares and contrasts aspects of their roles against that of the Commissioner for England.[25]

43. We heard from all three existing UK Commissioners during the course of our inquiry. Broadly speaking, while committed to working with the appointee for England, they told us that they foresaw the definition of the Children's Commissioner for England role as comparatively weak, and that there was a risk in consequence that the Commissioner for England would be a less effective champion than had been widely hoped for.

---

24   Discussed in section two of this report.

25   EVCM 64.

44. In addition, we are also mindful of the experience of countries outside the UK which have already established Children's and Young People's Commissioners. Norway and British Columbia, Canada are two cases in point, and our visits there in October 2004 and January 2005 respectively, provided us with the opportunity to learn from their experience. British Columbia appointed a Children's Commissioner in September 1996, following the recommendations of an inquiry into the death of Matthew John Vaudreuil in 1992. The remit was somewhat different from that of the English Commissioner—having a prime focus on investigating individual cases of child abuse. In 2002, following a change of Government, the office was disbanded and effectively replaced with a new Officer for Children and Youth in the context of a reorganisation of Governmental departments. Two reasons were offered for the disbanding of the post: first, it was felt that the original Commissioner's role duplicated the responsibilities of some other organisations and overlapped with some government departmental roles. Second, the relationship between the Commissioner and Ministers had sometimes been unproductively tense.

The Purpose of the Commissioner for England Role

45. The role of the Children's Commissioner for England is defined in statute as 'promoting awareness of the views and interests of children in England'. This differs from the remit of many other Children's Commissioners in Europe (including those in the devolved administrations) whose remits are framed in terms of promoting and protecting children's rights in accordance with the United Nations Convention on the Rights of the Child (UNCRC).

46. During the passage of the Children Bill through Parliament, the purpose of the Commissioner for England's role was the subject of extensive debate—with many commentators arguing that, as well as being out of keeping with existing Commissioners, anything other than a rights-based role would lead to a weak Commissioner who differed little in effect from children's charities. In the event, an amendment made to the Children Bill stipulated that the Children's Commissioner 'must have regard' to the United Nations Convention on the Rights of the Child in discharging his or her duties. **We have yet to be convinced that a Children's Commissioner, role primarily defined in terms of promoting children's views, will be as effective in practice as one focused on promoting and protecting children's rights in accordance with the United Nations Convention on the Rights of the Child.**

47. The lack of a rights-based remit for the Commissioner was a subject of concern to a very substantial number of those who submitted evidence to the inquiry, especially those from within the voluntary and charitable sectors.[26] The three existing UK Commissioners reaffirmed these views, and were also able to give us evidence of how the rights-based definition of their roles had influenced the operation of their office to date. They told us that the focus on rights had been crucial to the successful functioning of their role. The Commissioner for Scotland, Prof. Kathleen Marshall, explained that a rights-based focus had given her role moral authority and had been directly responsible for increasing her credibility with children:

---

26   Including EVCM 32, para. 6.2; EVCM 44 paras 4.1–4.3; EVCM 12, sect. 5.

"I started explaining it to children this way but I now explain it to adults this way because I think it gives it a moral authority, is I say that the UN Convention on the Rights of the Child, for example, is a set of promises that we have made to children, that we will do certain things to make life better for them. I think the fact we are saying we have made promises to them is something that children and young people understand, they understand about keeping promises and about failing to keep promises. Also, I think it is important to underline the fact that I do not make the rights up. The promises have already been made in our ratification of this international convention and my job, as I see it, is to keep the Government and the country to the promises that have already been made. I think that does give it very much a weight and an objective content. Interests can be subjective, people can have different views on the interests of children [...] I feel it is critical to my role in that moral authority to keep harping on about that thing that is objective, it is already promised and I am there to try and make the promises real."[27]

48. **We are concerned that the definition of the role of the Children's Commissioner for England as one primarily framed in terms of promoting children's views and concerns, rather than promoting and safeguarding rights, may directly and negatively affect the ability of the Commissioner to achieve improved outcomes for children and young people.** This is something that we intend to keep under review as the office is established and the Commissioner begins his activities.

Independence

49. Other concerns have focused on the likely independence of the Commissioner for England. The Children Act 2004 gives the Secretary of State powers to direct the Commissioner to conduct an inquiry into a particular subject. The appointee for England will also be under an obligation to consult with the Secretary of State before undertaking any inquiry or investigation. The potential for political interference worries many, and has been perceived as something which fundamentally undermines the neutrality and likely effectiveness of the role.

50. The power of the Secretary of State to direct inquiries or investigations is also at variance with the position of the existing UK Commissioners, who are under no obligation to consult with Ministers or carry out investigations on their request. The three existing appointees told us that they thought this section of the Act was inappropriate and had the potential to hinder the work of the Children's Commissioner for England. The Children's Commissioner for Wales, Peter Clarke, told the Committee:

"One thing that concerns me about the Secretary of State being able to instruct the English Commissioner to hold such an inquiry is I have a clear understanding now of how much time and resource it takes to conduct such a thing [...] I am very concerned that such an instruction would seriously silt up or make it unlikely that the Children's Commissioner for England would be able to do very much else, unless, of course, they go and ask what was the Lord Chancellor to lend them a judge to do the hearings, but then I do not understand why the Children's Commissioner

---

need be involved at all as the Government could do that on its own volition in any case or it could—as it did with Climbié—appoint somebody to do it."[28]

51. In oral evidence, the Minister explained to us that the circumstances in which the Secretary of State would require the Children's Commissioner for England to conduct a particular inquiry would be limited to cases where there had been "a particularly tragic set of circumstances round an individual child or a group of children, which requires a national inquiry—a Climbié-type inquiry."[29] The Minister also said that under no circumstances could the Secretary of State act to prevent the Commissioner from conducting any particular inquiry.[30] Looking to the future, she told us that she foresaw the relationship between Ministers and the Commissioner as one that would make her life "uncomfortable from time to time."[31]

52. **We welcome the Minister's assurance that the circumstances in which the Secretary of State will direct the Commissioner will be limited to very serious or tragic cases that require a national inquiry. We also welcome the assurance that the Secretary of State will under no circumstances prevent an inquiry being conducted. However, further clarification of the limits of directive powers should be made through regulation if necessary. Moreover, if there is no intention to ever prevent the Commissioner from conducting a particular inquiry, we fail to see the purpose of a duty to consult prior to launching an investigation. It is conceivable that future Secretaries of State may not take the same view, and we believe the Government should consider modifying this part of the Act.**

53. **It should be made clear at the earliest possible opportunity what level of funding will be available for the operation of the Commissioner's office and whether additional resources will be provided if the Secretary of State instructs the Commissioner to conduct a major inquiry which is likely to tie up large amounts of resources and personnel time—or whether it is expected that those costs will be met out of current allocations.**

54. **We are reassured to hear the Minister's assessment of her likely working relationship with the Children's Commissioner for England as one that was likely to be uncomfortable at times—in our view, anything less would be profoundly worrying, and as a Committee, we will look for evidence that the relationship between the Children's Commissioner and Ministers is developing in an appropriate way.**

Jurisdiction

55. Under statute, the Children's Commissioner for England will have responsibility for some crucial areas of policy affecting the lives of children in the devolved administrations - for example, in the case of Wales, criminal justice and home affairs which are matters

---

28   Q 230

29   Q 575

30   Q 577–8

31   Q 574

reserved to Westminster.[32] The existing UK Commissioners told us that they were concerned about the potential effect that overlapping remits would have on children – and in particular, on their understanding of the role of the Commissioner and their clarity about who to go to with their problems and anxieties. The Children's Commissioner for Scotland explained:

> "I think there is potential for confusion in having two Commissioners operating in each country. To me it does seem strange that, in a sense, it contradicts one of the aims of Every Child Matters which was to have one person in charge. We have created a system where, as far as the Commissioners are concerned, we have two people and we are going to have to be very careful about how that is publicised and how the message gets over to children and young people in our respective countries."[33]

56. Speaking on this issue, the Minister for Children has said previously that jurisdictional issues were something the Commissioners would need to 'sit down and sort [...] out among themselves.'[34] We put this to the three UK Commissioners, and they responded that they were indeed determined to work closely with the appointee for England to resolve these and any other difficulties. In written evidence, they stated that they "look forward to working with whoever is appointed to the post of English Commissioner for Children, and to drawing up with them a Memorandum (or possibly Memoranda) of Understanding to promote effective working between us all".[35]

57. **We are pleased that the three existing Commissioners are committed to working with the Commissioner for England to resolve any problems concerning jurisdiction. Their suggestion that a memorandum of understanding should be drawn up at the earliest possible convenience seems a productive way forward, and is one possible way to broach issues of jurisdiction. This would also provide an opportunity to capitalise on the valuable experience of the three existing Commissioners—which they are extremely keen to share with the appointee for England.**

58. In conclusion, we are concerned that the legal framework for the Children's Commissioner for England role may place undue constraints on his ability to be a force for change for children in practice. It is essential that the Commissioner for England is viewed—not least by children and young people—as a powerful champion who operates completely free from political interference. The Children's Commissioner for Wales told us he has recently set in train a review of the effectiveness of his office and this seems to us a useful precedent.

59. **We suggest that a fully independent review of the role and remit of the Children's Commissioner for England should be commissioned within three years of appointment. This should include analysis of the effectiveness of the Commissioner post, with particular reference to the impact of the statutory framework. Amendments**

---

32 The Children's Commissioner for England will also be entitled (or could be instructed by the Secretary of State) to conduct inquiries or investigations relating to reserved policy in Wales, Northern Ireland and Scotland.

33 Q 228

34 epolitix.com, *Hodge dismisses fears of Wales' Children's Commissioner*, 27 December 2004.

35 EVCM 64, para 5.

to statute should be pursued if the review indicates that the Children's Commissioner is unduly constrained by the existing legal framework.

60. To preserve independence of the Children's Commissioner for England, there needs to be a strong link between the Commissioner and Parliament. By custom and practice Her Majesty's Chief Inspector of Schools reports directly to Parliament through this Committee and we envisage a similar relationship with the Children's Commissioner for England.

5 Integrated services at the front line

Integrated front line teams—a clear vision?

61. The Government intends that as a result of *Every Child Matters*, closer professional working will become more widespread and integrated front line teams (including staff from health, education, social services and other agencies) will increasingly become the norm. The aim of integrated teams at the front line is ostensibly to enable a more seamless service to be provided to children and young people, in a more holistic way than is currently the case, bringing together universal and more targeted services. This aim attracted widespread support in the oral and written evidence we have received, as it did in the consultation responses to the original *Every Child Matters* Green Paper.

62. To date, there has been relatively little centrally-generated guidance on the likely constitution and day to-day operation of integrated front line teams, although there has been some guidance on how Children's Centres are to operate and be governed,[36] as well as evidence from the evaluation of Early Excellence Centres which describes some characteristics of integrated teams.[37] The lack of overt prescription on the part of the DfES fits with a general approach which advocates local discretion. In their written evidence, they state:

> "Integrated working will take a variety of forms depending on the needs of children and families locally—from virtual teams brought together around the needs of particular children through to fully co-located multi-agency teams made up of professionals from different disciplines and organisations."[38]

63. Here, the 'local direction' versus 'central leadership' tension is again apparent, with some clearly feeling that current conceptualisations of multidisciplinary teams are too vague. The Royal College of Nurses, for example, wrote that they were:

> "concerned that there is not a clearer vision from Government of how multidisciplinary teams will be constituted in practice. The move towards a duty to collaborate is welcomed by the RCN however we feel that on a practical level it is important to develop a model of how integration will work in practice. The model should not be overly prescriptive but greater clarity is required to provide guidance to professionals on how they should work together on a day to day basis."[39]

64. While we would contend strongly that there are many valuable lessons to be learned from current multi-disciplinary practice, especially with regard to Sure Start and existing Children's Centres, we agree that a clearer central vision on how multi-disciplinary teams might be constituted and operated in day-to-day practice is needed. Building on existing models of interagency working is no doubt a positive way forward, but there are areas of

---

36   Department for Education and Skills/ Sure Start Unit *Children's Centres—Developing integrated services for young children and their families. Start-up guidance*, 2004.

37   See Bertram et. al., *Early Excellence Centre Pilot Programme: Third Annual Evaluation Report 2001-2002*, 2002Centre for Research in Early Childhood, St Thomas Centre, Birmingham/ Sure Start Unit.

38   EVCM 58, para 32.

39   EVCM 5, para 2.2.

the country where there will be a shorter history of multidisciplinary working and less, therefore, to build on. Exemplars, or the circulation of best practice, could be of assistance in these areas and may provide the stimulation necessary to bring about innovation on the ground. We understand that guidance on multi-agency working will be published in April 2005 and we welcome this. It is easy to under-estimate the practical complexities of moving towards co-located, multi-disciplinary teams, and we are concerned that some localities may interpret the absence of direction as a licence to avoid the issue entirely.

Lead professional

65. *Every Child Matters* proposes that multi-disciplinary teams will be led by a Lead Professional who will co-ordinate support for the child and serve as a point of contact. While again there is generalised support for the concept of a Lead Professional and agreement with the aims of such a role, criticism has focused on the lack of conceptualisation to date of how this role will operate in practice. This has led to some understandable worry, with some representative organisations concerned that the Lead Professional role may impose significant extra responsibility and a heavier workload on the selected person. The Association of Teachers and Lecturers wrote that with regard to teachers in particular:

> "it is absolutely correct to see the teacher as the first point of contact, [but] the consequence of the Workload Agreement is to sharpen the focus of what teachers should do to emphasise the classroom and teaching [...] The lead professional role is different in nature. We can envisage teachers accessing the necessary support *from* a lead professional rather than as a general rule undertaking that role."[40]

66. While we do not believe at all that it is the DfES's intention to 'foist' the lead professional role on teachers and other school staff, the ATL submission does resonate with other evidence we have heard about the potential workload and responsibility implications of the Lead Professional role. Inter-professional working is a notoriously complex area and the Lead Professional role will require sensitive handling. In particular it needs to be decided if the role is primarily one of service co-ordination or professional leadership, but in either case there will be important implications for training and development, capacity, resources and authority to act. We note that one of the findings from the early evaluation of the Information Sharing and Assessment trailblazer pilots was unwillingness to take on the Lead Professional role because of the workload implications, and thought needs to be given as to whether such a role is a new post or simply a 'bolt-on' to existing responsibilities.[41] If it is to be the latter, we are concerned that it may not be undertaken effectively; if the former, we need to know the resource implications and how they will be met. Draft guidance on the nature and operation of the Lead Professional role was published in March 2005. This has been developed in consultation with authorities that are already involved in integrated service provision at the front line, and goes some way to recognising and addressing the issues raised above.

---

40   EVCM 23, para 23.

41   Department for Education and Skills,.*Developing Information-Sharing and Assessment Systems*, Cleaver et. Al, 2004.

Co-location

67. *Every Child Matters* proposes that closer professional integration should be underpinned where appropriate by the co-location of services on single sites more accessible to children, young people and their families. Witnesses concurred with the potential benefits of such an approach, but even some of those in favour warned of the danger of seeing co-location as an end in itself. John Coughlan, representing the Association of Directors of Social Services (ADSS) told us:

> "I have certainly worked in circumstances where co-location has been achieved, but the different agencies did not know where each other's door was and could not walk round and get to each other. We have to be realistic and work on some of the frameworks." [42]

Chief Constable Terry Grange, representing the Association of Chief Police Officers, added:

> "as others have said, you need to think through the issues and the outcomes you intend. If co-location gets you there, fine, but for many organisations that will not be financially or geographically viable." [43]

68. Extended Schools and Sure Start Children's Centres have been advanced as examples of existing co-located services and it is intended that more of these facilities will be rolled out as *Every Child Matters* is implemented. Again, it seems to us entirely sensible to use current successful examples of co-location on the ground as a starting point for further development. There is good evidence that co-located services in schools and other 'non-traditional' environments are often perceived by parents, children and young people as less stigmatising and more accessible. Additionally, emerging research evaluations of Sure Start and Extended Schools[44] undoubtedly suggest that co-located services can have successful outcomes and there is further positive evidence available from the longer experience of such arrangements in adult services spanning health and social care.[45]

69. We do however have some reservations about the universal applicability of the school-based service model. As the YMCA and the Foyer Federation rightly stressed, any service located in or near a school will be, by definition, unattractive to many of the most vulnerable and excluded young people:

> "The concept of extended schools should not be 'overstretched'. Some young people are excluded from schools and it is unlikely that they will want to return to, or be welcome at, school premises 'after hours'. Furthermore many young people, while not excluded from school, nevertheless have considerable anxieties around school."[46]

---

42   Q 164

43   Q 166

44   ibid

45   *Primary Health Care and Social Care: Working Across professional Boundaries.* Hudson, B. et al Nuffield Institute for Health, University of Leeds, 2000.

46   EVCM 20, para 14.

"We have reservations about Extended Schools being used as a panacea to address a plethora of issues. Inter-agency working focused around a school site will fail to reach the majority of the 10,000 young people Foyers work with each year—arguably some of the most in need of help. It is therefore crucial that Government looks creatively about ways of providing alternative hubs for young people to access support services, and this should include engaging with the voluntary sector."[47]

70. When we asked the DfES about this issue, they acknowledged that services based around schools would not always be appropriate for all:

"There is a distinction between the service being provided actually on the school site and the school acting as a gateway to the people who can help that child and family in whatever way is most appropriate to them. Sometimes they may feel comfortable accessing some sort of support through school; sometimes it may be a very special need which is actually more sensible to provide centrally so I think there is going to be a different sort of pattern. One of the things we do not want to do—again because it is much more sensible for it to be worked out locally—is to define very precisely what the exact pattern of services will be for any individual school."[48]

71. As we have stated elsewhere, we are generally supportive of the intention to let local areas configure services as best suits local need, rather than follow a prescriptive model. However, we think that the Government needs to provide clearer guidance on the issue of co-location, emphasising the benefits of such an approach but also the steps which should precede a decision to co-locate. In the absence of further guidance, there is a risk that some areas will see the challenges of co-location as insurmountable.

72. **The DfES told us that they would shortly launch a prospectus on Extended Schools. Where conversion to an Extended School is being considered, we recommend that the prospectus should stress the benefits of planning with local partners, including voluntary services, who often have wide experience of engaging vulnerable groups, to ensure local needs are met.**

Workforce development and training needs

Tackling the 'silo mentality'; basic training

73. *Every Child Matters—Change for Children* recognises that "delivering more integrated services requires new ways of working and significant culture change for staff used to working within narrower professional and service-based boundaries."[49] The challenge of tackling entrenched cultures of working has resonated particularly strongly with many during the course of this inquiry. While there was extremely strong support in principle for the idea of integration at the front line, and many references to existing examples of good practice, the evidence stressed that the enduring challenge of bringing about culture change will be one of the most difficult to overcome, while also being one of the most important to achieve.

---

47   EVCM 29.

48   Q 416

49   ibid, pp 17.

74. The DfES foresees that the process of breaking down professional barriers will be addressed in a number of ways, including through basic multi-agency training provided at the local level—which they were keen to stress was already taking place on the ground:

> "The experience in our information sharing trailblazers, for example in some of our other pilot projects has shown the huge value to be gained by practitioners and professionals from different sectors—social workers, teachers, nurses—getting together in the same room and thereby effectively doubling the value of the training because not only do they learn about the skill that they were in the room specifically to learn about but they also learn about starting to build those relationships that are going to be so important to making this agenda work on the ground."[50]

75. We agree that there does seem to be evidence of positive experience from existing practice. As well as occurring through the Pathfinder and pilot projects as outlined above, interdisciplinary training has been taking place for some years in relation to Extended Schools initiatives, Sure Start programmes, Children's Centres and in health and welfare settings. These provide useful models and experience to learn from, but we do have some concerns about resource implications. Inter-disciplinary training and development take a great deal of planning and implementation, and also require capacity to be found both for funding the activity and releasing staff from their everyday duties, a matter which we discuss in more detail below (see: *funding of workforce development*, below).

Integrated working and professional identities

76. An issue linked to the matters identified above, which we discussed in some detail with witnesses, is the likely transformation of professional identities, responsibilities and specialist skills in a context of multi-disciplinary working. The main debate here has been about the extent to which integrated team working will imply a loss of specialism and discrete 'professions'. At the beginning of our inquiry, Lord Laming outlined some of the complex challenges of multi-agency working, stressing the importance of maintaining distinctions between professionals:

> "I believe very much in specialism, specialist knowledge and specialist skills. The idea that a social worker can be an expert in mental health, learning disabilities, the needs of elderly people and children, is fundamentally wrong. I would like to see social workers being expert in their particular field, and that means knowing the legislation, knowing what their role is, having confidence in the systems, and being clear about the responsibilities of other agencies. Secondly, I do not think that social services should be treated as the catch-all; that when there are problems for other services, if they refer the child to social services that means they can abdicate their responsibilities. Every one of them has a unique and distinctive responsibility, and a continuing responsibility, whether it is in the Health Service – whether it is a GP, a health visitor or a police officer."[51]

77. This emphasis on the retention of specialist skills is echoed in recent DfES communications:

---

50   Q 422

51   Q 23

"Multi-disciplinary working helps to ensure that children, young people and their families are given swift and simple access to the complementary skills of a wide range of people working together. It is not about losing the benefit of individual specialisms, although joint working may lead to some remodelling of roles."[52]

Philip Collins, Director, Social Market Foundation, told us that he saw this remodelling of professional roles and identities as one of the biggest challenges to successful integrated working at the front line:

"This is going to be a very significant problem when we try and integrate this profession. For example, the tensions between people who see themselves as educators, people who see themselves as carers are already looming. I do not think at the moment there is a very clear way through that problem. Those professional demarcations I think are going to prove to be extremely hard to negotiate [...] the original vision of the Bill in the Act, in the Green Paper, I think was to envisage moving from a social care workforce and health workforce to a children's workforce. It is now unclear to me whether that is still where we are going. The position of health visitors and midwives, for example, is made much more complicated by this process because their hope and aim is simply to carry on in their neatly defined professional package and be part of a multi-disciplinary team. If instead we head towards something like a children's practitioner, everybody is in some way a children's practitioner with their specialisms underneath and that alters the nature of those professionals quite markedly in ways which as yet we have not thought through seriously. Trying to think through what the integration of service means for people's jobs is very, very important."[53]

78. While we would contest the assertion that health visitors and midwives are particularly resistant to any redefinition of their professional functions,[54] the point about the need for further consideration of likely transformations of professional roles is well made. **A toolkit on multi-agency working is scheduled to be released in April 2005—and we will be interested to see what prominence is given to challenges around the reconfiguring of professional identities and responsibilities that working in a multi-agency team is likely to present.**

79. We recognise and welcome the work that is being carried out by the DfES on the development of a 'common core of skills and knowledge'[55] which, it is intended, will be integrated into initial training programmes across a range of disciplines. The key issue now is implementation, and we will monitor the changes that are being made to initial training programmes in response to the 'common core'. Additionally, we note that the new Children's Workforce Development Council is soon to become operational, and that part of its remit will be to 'play a key role in supporting local services in workforce planning and workforce development.'[56] Inter-agency training for in-service staff across different

---

52 Department for Education and Skills, *Every Child Matters: Change for Children*, para. 3.19, p 17, 2004.

53 Q 51–52

54 Evidence from the evaluation of Sure Start programmes has demonstrated that nurses and health visitors have been key players in multi-disciplinary teams, and have often changed their practice significantly as a result.

55 Seehttp://www.dfes.gov.uk/commoncore/ or more information on the Common Core of Skills and Knowledge.

56 Department for Education and Skills, *Every Child Matters: Change for Children*, para 3.25, p. 18, 2004.

professions will be vital if *Every Child Matters'* goals are to be achieved. As with reforms to initial training programmes, we will be monitoring the extent to which inter-agency training is taking place on the ground.

80. The likely professional role of teachers and other school staff in inter-disciplinary teams has been less well defined than most. The original *Every Child Matters* Green Paper identified a list of professionals who might increasingly work together in teams clustered around the child. This list included schools support staff and school nurses but, as Peter Moss, Professor of Early Childhood Provision, Institute of Education and colleagues note, it did not refer to teachers or the school leadership. This, it is argued, is indicative of a wider conceptual problem:

> "the school workforce is treated separately from the remainder of the workforce engaged with children, both conceptually and structurally. Although teachers are one of the most numerous groups working with children, they do not appear in para 4.26 of the Green Paper as one of the groups of "professionals and non-professionals [who] might increasingly work together in different types of teams". Within the DfES, there is a Children's Workforce Unit and a Schools Workforce Unit. At the same time, responsibility for training teachers and others working with children is hived off to different organisations, albeit loosely connected through a 'UK Children's Workforce Network'."[57]

81. This should be a concern not least because the school workforce – and teachers in particular—are in close and extended contact with most children. The DfES told us that they were currently working with the Teacher Training Agency to integrate child protection and other relevant skills training into initial teacher training programmes, as part of the drive to ensure that all those working with children received training in a common core of skills. Additionally, the Department told us that the training of in-service teachers would be monitored by Local Safeguarding Children Boards[58] which would have a general remit to assess what types of training were most needed in their local areas. However, we would contend that the ability of Local Safeguarding Children Boards to ensure in-service training is available to all teachers will depend directly on the ability and willingness of schools to resource such training—an issue about which we have significant concerns and which we discuss in more detail below.

82. We hope that the Extended Schools prospectus currently in development will contain clear guidance, underpinned by clear concepts, about how school staff might work alongside others in multidisciplinary teams. **The introduction of an integrated inspection framework offers a further opportunity to emphasise the importance of integrated working at the front line, and we hope the final guidance on integrated inspection later this year will focus in part on this issue.** Further, the framework for individual institution inspections carried out by Ofsted is currently being revised to ensure that schools are assessed on the extent to which they help children attain the five 'outcomes' of *Every Child*

57   EVCM 16

58   Statutory Local Safeguarding Children Boards (LSCBs) should be in place in all areas by 2006. LSCBs will replace Area Child Protection Committees where these previously existed.

Matters.[59] Conceivably, such inspections could comment specifically upon whether teachers have access to the in-service training (for example, in safeguarding or working with professionals in other disciplines) necessary to support children and young people to attain the five outcomes.

Managerial competency

83. Integrated and multi-disciplinary teams—especially where co-located and therefore with staff working outside traditional 'disciplinary' environments—raise specific challenges as regards ensuring that appropriate managerial and professional supervision is in place. Front line practitioners and professional organisations told us of their concerns in this area. For example, the Association of Directors of Education and Children's Services told us that there was a need to:

> "look again at line management questions, the ways in which we can safely operate inter-disciplinary teams, and at the same time keep the professional supervision tight and of high quality so that people being part of those teams will continue to be professionally developed and continue to be able to practise their skills safely."[60]

84. Similarly, the Royal College of Nurses argued that:

> "For nursing staff working within integrated teams it is vitally important that they have access to professional leadership. When establishing integrated teams there should be clear lines of professional accountability and nurses should be able to easily access continuing professional development, clinical supervision and practice development, even though they are working as part of a collaborative team."[61]

85. For their part, the DfES recognise the need for professionals in multidisciplinary or integrated teams to be appropriately supported and managed. Draft statutory guidance on Children's Trusts[62] clarifies that professionals in these teams should have access to continuous professional development, appropriate clinical and professional supervision and management which offers clear lines of accountability. This said, there does not appear to date to be a fully coherent plan for the development of service managers' skills at the national level. This is not to say that there is no such work going on. The General Teaching Council noted that the National College for School Leadership (NCSL) has:

> "already embarked on potentially exciting work to capture the leadership and management demands of extended schools, and integrated children's centres. This work rightly emphasises the need for leaders with advanced skills in co-ordinating services including those beyond their own professional sphere, and being

---

59 The Children Bill 2005, which is before Parliament at the time of writing, extends the remit of Ofsted to look at how far institutions contribute to the well-being of children. Well-being is defined with reference to the five 'outcomes' of Every Child Matters.

60 Q 164

61 EVCM 5, para 3.3.

62 Department for Education and Skills, *[Draft] Statutory Guidance on interagency co-operation to improve the wellbeing of children: Children's Trusts*, 2004.

entrepreneurial and innovative in identifying human, material and financial resources that support wide objectives for children and young people."[63]

This work has been used to inform the development of a National Professional Qualification in Integrated Centre Leadership, for which the DfES has been an advisory partner and which we understand will be rolled out in September 2005.[64] We will be interested to learn whether attainment of this qualification will become mandatory for managers of integrated service settings.

86. The DfES is currently drafting its Children's Pay and Workforce Strategy and the new Sector Skills Council dedicated to the Children's Workforce is about to become operational. We hope that these will place a high priority on supporting both the development of generic managerial skills and professional supervisory skills among those who manage front line workers—especially those in multi-disciplinary teams.

Funding of workforce development

87. In general terms it is expected that the associated training needs of *Every Child Matters* for in-service staff will have to be found from existing budgets. The DfES told us that:

> "There are already resources on the ground for training and what we will be expecting and wanting local agencies to do is to bend those training opportunities so that they are taking account of the changed agenda".[65]

88. The DfES told us that some money to support workforce development had been had been factored into the change funds and safeguarding children grants[66] that were being made available to local areas—but local areas would ultimately be responsible for deciding priorities for spending of their allocation. In the case of the Department of Health, funding for the *Every Child Matters/ National Service Framework* agenda would principally come, we were told, through Primary Care Trust allocations—and this applied to funding for training as well[67].

89. **We are not convinced that workforce training needs for all in-service staff are likely to be given the priority across the board at the local level that they merit and which the Government anticipates. While we appreciate that there are significant resources already invested in the training of children's professionals in some sectors, we are particularly concerned about the priority which will be attached to *Every Child Matters*—related workforce development for staff in other sectors, and particularly the health services.**

90. **Department of Health officials told us that there was no ring-fenced money at departmental level for training[68]. With little or no extra resources identified for the**

---

63   EVCM 31, para. 13.

64   See *National Professional Qualification in Integrated Centre Leadership Pilot Programme—Frequently Asked Questions*, available at http://www.ncsl.org.uk/mediastore/image2/npqicl-faqs.pdf

65   Q 425

66   See section eight of this report for details of Change Funds and Safeguarding Children grants.

67   Qq 393, 397, 398.

68   Q 424

implementation of *Every Child Matters* in general, we are concerned that with many pressures on Primary Care Trusts and other budgets, crucial *Every Child Matters*—related training will not be given the priority it deserves.

91. The Association of Directors of Education and Children's Services (ADECS) has suggested that all staff working in children's services should have an entitlement to three days' basic training, which might cover building understanding of the new service context, learning new protocols and procedures, and team building.[69] They were sceptical that the cost of meeting such an entitlement could easily be met from existing budgets and suggested instead that the Government might consider developing an entitlement approach to basic training, underpinned by a pooled budget between the DfES and Department of Health. Officials, however, indicated that there were no plans to develop such a pooled inter-departmental training budget and did not think that an entitlement approach was appropriate.[70]

92. **We would urge that the presumption against an entitlement to training—with a pooled fund at interdepartmental level to support it—is reconsidered. Such a move would send out clear signals to local areas that training and workforce development were being given a high priority, and would also provide vital initial resources to address some of the staff development and training needs arising from the implementation of the *Every Child Matters* agenda.**

69   EVCM 15.

70   Qq 421, 424

6 Integrated processes

Child indexes/databases

93. As part of measures to improve communication between professionals, and ultimately outcomes for children and young people, the DfES intends to implement IT-based, multi-agency index(es) containing basic details on all children in the country. This has been one of the most controversial aspects of the *Every Child Matters* reforms, and one that has consistently attracted strong criticism in both written and oral evidence.

94. The rationale for the index(es) is briefly summarised as follows—it will serve as a tool to:

- help practitioners identify quickly a child with whom they have contact, and whether that child is getting the universal services (education, primary health care) to which he or she is entitled;

- enable earlier identification of needs and earlier and more effective action to address them by providing a tool for practitioners to identify who else is involved with or has a concern about a child; and

- encourage better communication and closer working between different professionals and practitioners.[71]

95. The failure of other recent Government-funded IT-based initiatives, some commissioned by the DfES, makes us more cautious than might otherwise be the case about these proposals. This Committee has recently inquired into two other projects—the UK e-University venture and Individual Learning Accounts. The first of these failed to achieve its ends and has consumed £53 million of public funds, while the second collapsed under suspicion of fraud and an overspend of £60 million. Consequently, the development of child indexes needs to be approached with the utmost caution, not least because it would be unreasonable to expect the taxpayer to bear the cost of another IT failure.

Initial development work on the indexes—context

96. In 2002, six Local authority areas or groupings of areas (since expanded to ten) were selected to become Identification, Referral and Tracking Trailblazers, now re-branded as Information Sharing and Assessment Trailblazers (ISAs). Each was provided with £1 million to test and develop ways of improving co-ordination and information-sharing between agencies involved with children and young people. The work being carried out includes: clarification of how and when practitioners should share information; development of child indexes or databases; development of a common assessment framework (CAF) and a range of activities to support better information sharing within and across children's services. A team from the Royal Holloway College, University of London, led by Prof. Hedy Cleaver, were commissioned to analyse the initial development of Information Sharing and Assessment Trailblazers and analysis of the development of

---

71 Summary adapted from DfES Information Sharing and Assessment website,
    http://www.dfes.gov.uk/ISA/IndexProp/indexProp.cfm

child indexes took place as part of this project. The researchers completed collecting evidence in August 2004, and their report was published in November 2004[72].

Will child indexes improve outcomes for children?

97. The development of child indexes is potentially extremely costly. We have received a number of different estimates of the resources—up to £1 billion pounds in one case—that are likely to be needed for initial development and maintenance. However, when we asked the Minister about development costs, we were told that the estimate of £1 billion was "absurd", and that the real figure would be in "the low hundreds" of millions of pounds[73].

98. Unarguably, several hundred million pounds remains a very significant amount of money. A key consideration must be whether it is justifiable to spend such a large sum on the development of child indexes when there are other very substantial calls on funding and, more importantly, other available ways of fostering improved communication between professionals—for example, through multi-agency training which can develop a culture of openness and trust between traditionally separate professionals. The evidence we have received has left us with doubts about whether investment in child indexes can currently be justified in terms of the contribution it is likely to make to improving outcomes for children.

99. Professor Cleaver told us that almost all the Trailblazers, at the end of the research period, had functioning index systems or had such systems in development and were preparing for imminent implementation. On the likely value of these systems, she has written that "outcomes for children will be improved if practitioners communicate and services are delivered in a co-ordinated way. A child index with details of how to contact other practitioners could aid this process but must not be seen as the whole solution".[74] Dr. Eileen Munro, London School of Economics told us categorically, however, that she did not think investment in improving information-sharing in general and indexes in particular was justifiable, especially in the light of other pressing demands on resources:

> "in talking about information-sharing as being a crucial aspect in good work, people are misunderstanding the mistakes that have been made in the child protection cases. In the case of Victoria Climbié there was no shortage of information but there was a shortage of wisdom of how to understand that information. Giving those workers even more information would make them less competent than they were. It is not the answer; it is about improving the workforce."[75]

She went on to explain further:

> "In Victoria Climbié's case it was not a question of them [professionals] not knowing how many other people had been involved, but not seeing the significance of it.

---

72   Ibid

73   Qq 565, 566

74   Department for Education and Skills, Cleaver *et. al.* '*Developing Information Sharing and Assessment Systems*', pp. 68, 2004.

75   Q 322

There was no secret about her hospital visits. The Haringey social worker knew about the Brent involvement. It was that the brain cells did not operate."[76]

100. It is clear that there are several specific and interrelated operational challenges which will need to be successfully overcome if there is to be any prospect of child indexes serving as the useful professional tool that the Government envisages. We address some of these specific challenges below, dealing in turn with: registering 'flags of concern' and contact with sensitive services; security; ensuring the accuracy of information held; and a source for the 'unique identifier'.

'Flags of concern' and the recording of sensitive information

101. The DfES has proposed that electronic 'flags of concern' should be attached where appropriate to children's files. These flags would serve as a means of alerting other practitioners, thus building up a more complete picture of the circumstances of the child. They would then serve as a trigger for contacting other professionals. It is also proposed that where children have contact with additional—often specialist—services the contact details of the practitioner should be placed on the file—again, enabling practitioners involved with the same child to contact each other.

102. These two aspects of the proposed indexes have been seen as inherently problematic by a very large number who have given evidence on the topic, including the Information Commissioner, Richard Thomas[77]. We were especially interested to hear that Professor Cleaver shared these concerns, based on her own analysis of trailblazer authorities. She told us:

> "The more complicated they [the indexes] get, and the more information put on, i.e., flags of concern, or even the names of the agencies working with the child, you will have difficulties because agencies like CAMHS [Child and Adolescent Mental Health Services] or the Brook Clinic signal more information than you need, and those are the agencies that do not want themselves to be put on. If you go that route you will get into all sorts of complications. The research would suggest the simpler the better."[78]

103. The DfES responded to these concerns—which have been expressed over a long period—by issuing a consultation on this aspect of the database. The Government response to this consultation has not yet been released, so we are unable to be sure at this stage what plans are being made in this area, although the Minister did tell us that "the key to this [the child indexes in general] is simplicity, and I am determined to have that."[79] We take this—and the consultation—as positive signs that concerns over the adding of flags of concern and practitioner details are being taken extremely seriously, but nevertheless, we think that the Government should aim to clarify their intentions in this area as soon as is feasible.

---

76   Q 326

77   See EVCM 66. Here, the Information Commissioner lays out a detailed response to the ongoing consultation.

78   Q 322

79   Q 543

104. A further concern here is that the use of a flag should indicate that a professional has a 'cause for concern', but what constitutes such a concern is left undefined and seen as a matter for professional judgement. Since professional groups work to diverse definitions and interpretations, there is unlikely to be a consensus on meaning. This could lead to an unnecessary volume of information on the database and a consequent diversion of professional energies from real concerns. The information Commissioner shares this concern, noting in his written evidence that practitioners may simply add a flag of concern as a defensive measure to ensure they are legally covered.[80] This in turn could trigger superfluous work and may lead to undue intervention in a child or young person's life. We feel there needs to be a much clearer and shared understanding of what constitutes a cause for concern and urge the DfES to clarify this matter before the indexes become operational.

Security

105. The security of information on IT-based indexes has also been a major concern for those submitting evidence—and for us as a Committee. Inappropriate access and retrieval of information by those looking to harm children clearly risks undermining the ultimate aim of the indexes—to protect and safeguard children's and young people's welfare. Women's Aid, for example, told us that they were: "concerned that electronic databases specified in the current Children Bill could be used by abusers to track down women and children fleeing from domestic violence, and recommend that appropriate safeguards are introduced into these systems as a matter of urgency."[81]

106. In oral evidence, we were told by Professor Hedy Cleaver that research carried out by Trailblazer authorities with children themselves had revealed that many had serious concerns about the potential for data to serve, paradoxically, as a 'resource' for those looking to harm them. Professor Cleaver explained:

> "They [the children] just did not believe all those wise words of the Government, saying it would be secure. They just did not believe it and they wanted very little information kept on those databases because they were frightened that paedophiles would find out, particularly if there was a flag of concern. You can identify vulnerable children, because there was the name, the age of the child and the school they went to, so that you could go and visit, and there was a concern; so you knew immediately that this was a vulnerable child— "goody, goody". They were very concerned about that."[82]

107. Evidence from the Information Sharing and Assessment Trailblazers further showed, however, that the issue of security is one that has been taken extremely seriously by those trialling systems, and a number of technical and other solutions have been piloted in different circumstances—including, for example, the necessity to enter a series of passwords and other personal information before being able to access records. While we would not contend that security presents an insurmountable problem, we would argue that

---

80   EVCM 66

81   EVCM 34, para 2.4.

82   Q 364

existing publicly available analysis of child indexes does not demonstrate beyond doubt that workable solutions have been found.

Monitoring and ensuring accuracy of information on the databases

108. Much of the evidence we have heard has stressed the importance of keeping information on the database accurate and up to date—otherwise its value as a source of information will be undermined. It is clear that potentially disastrous consequences could ensue should outdated information be retained on the system when circumstances change. The Information Commissioner outlined to us a case whereby details about a child had changed but these had not been updated on the records:

> "a father was alleged to have been abusing his child. Another person was then prosecuted for that matter and the father was entirely innocent, and yet the records were not updated, and that was still there against that particular parent's name. It is fundamental not just to keep track of the names and addresses, but to keep track of the changes of circumstances as the various processes move forward.".[83]

109. The Information Commissioner went on to point out that the administrative burden of keeping indexes fully up to date should not be underestimated. The risk to children and their families posed by the potential for storage of false or outdated information should therefore be assessed as the Government moves to produce its business case on the indexes—and there should be clear, transparent explanations of how the administrative burdens of updating the system would be met.

Unique identifying number

110. A network of child indexes depends for operational integrity on the association of a unique identifier with each child's record, in order to ensure that data retrieved or entered relates to the appropriate child and that there is no confusion between, for example, children with the same name. Almost all of the evidence we have received on this subject—including that from the Department itself—has indicated that finding such a unique identifier is in practice proving to be extremely difficult. In oral evidence, Officials told us that that they were currently involved in discussions with Ministers and colleagues about the issue and were due to present a recommendation to the cross-departmental Committee of Ministers in April 2005. We appreciate that this is not something which can be subject to a 'quick fix'. It has to be a cause for concern that at this late stage in proceedings, a source for the unique identifier has not been decided upon.

111. Although the Minister sought to reassure us that she would not proceed to the commissioning stage until she was certain that indexes were "not going to be an IT disaster, but [...] a good additional tool,"[84] we remain concerned about the development of child indexes and would urge the Government to proceed with the very utmost caution in this area. The Minister has confirmed that further research will be commissioned to

---

83   Q 365

84   Q 568

examine the impact of indexes in Trailblazer areas, the findings of which would be used to inform the business case for implementation,[85] and we welcome this.

112. **In the past, this committee has been concerned that crucial policy decisions are sometimes taken without sufficient research or evaluation of existing practice. In this case, the fundamental decision to go ahead with child indexes appears to have been taken before the activities of the Information Sharing and Assessment Trailblazers could be fully analysed.**

113. **We are not convinced that sufficient evidence currently exists to justify the commissioning of the proposed IT-based child indexes. We have significant reservations about whether this will represent the best use of resources and very significant concerns about critical issues such as security, confidentiality and access arrangements. We are concerned in particular that the current research evidence does not conclusively demonstrate that expenditure in this area is the best way of improving outcomes for children.**

114. **We welcome the news that further evaluative work on the impact of indexes in Trailblazer areas is now being planned, and that the results of this will be used to inform the business case for implementation. This research should analyse the comparative benefit of the indexes as a means of improving outcomes and other ways of improving information-sharing within and between professionals.**

Common Assessment Framework

115. Along with child indexes, the development and implementation of the Common Assessment Framework (CAF) is a key means of achieving closer integration of services at the process level. It aims is to "provide a national, common process for early assessment to identify more accurately and speedily the additional needs of children and young people".[86] Specifically, the CAF aims to:

- "provide an easy-to-use assessment of all the child's individual, family and community needs, which can be built up over time and, with consent, shared between Practitioners […] ;

- improve the quality of referrals between agencies by making them more evidence-based;

- help embed a common language about the needs of children and young people;

- promote the appropriate sharing of information; and reduce the number and duration of different assessment processes which children and young people need to undergo."[87]

116. The Children Act 1989 defines two sets of circumstances where assessments and interventions should be carried out. On the one hand, Section 17 lays out the need for assessment where children are in need. Section 47 defines the duty to carry out assessment/

---

85   EVCM 74

86   Department for Education and Skills, *Every Child Matters. Change for Children*, para 3.29, p 18, 2004.

87   Department for Education and Skills, *Every Child Matters. Change for Children*, para 3.31, p 19, 2004.

intervention where a child is thought to be in need of protection. The Common Assessment Framework has been widely perceived as a means to align different agency assessment procedures, but it can also be understood as a method of bringing together sections 17 and 47 of the Children Act 1989.

117. Information Sharing and Assessment Trailblazer authorities were charged with developing common assessment processes as part of their activities. Trailblazers' experience has fed into the design of the national Common Assessment Framework, which was issued in first draft form for consultation in August 2004 and was subsequently released as draft guidance subject to refinement in January 2005.[88] It is expected that the guidance will be issued in its final format by April 2006 so all Local Authorities can begin implementation.

118. While we have encountered very widespread support for the aims and objectives of the CAF, and the potential benefits it could provide, we are also aware of concerns about the lack of clarity surrounding its final form and the ways in which it will be used in practice. This is no doubt inevitable given that CAF is still in the final stages of development, and there is clearly a trade-off to be made between valuing consultation as a means of developing policy and the benefits of providing a clear sense of direction and certainty from the very outset. We have also been told of concerns about particular operational issues, many of which resonate with discussions about the implementation of other aspects of the *Every Child Matters* programme, including: pressures on the workforce; the cost of training staff in its use and the cost of implementation; ensuring take-up of the CAF; and the link between assessment and entitlement to assistance. In the main, these issues were also, unsurprisingly, raised by agencies who responded to the consultation carried out in late 2004.

Implications for workload and costs of staff training.

119. The introduction of the CAF has inevitably raised concern among some about the potential impact on the workload of those who will be expected to incorporate it into their professional practice. Additionally, training in the use of CAF will need to be provided for those staff that are expected to use it in day-to-day practice. The LGA comments on both of these issues:

> "If the common assessment framework is to be effective particularly in universal settings such as schools, additional training of staff will be needed. Consideration will also be required as to which staff would have the skills to undertake such an assessment. There could also be workload implications as a result. The framework should add value and not be seen as additional bureaucracy if it is to achieve its aim. These issues link into the wider children's workforce skills and training developments."[89]

120. In the draft guidance, the DfES proposes a number of ways of addressing the costs of training and potential impact on workload. With regard to the former, it proposes: a phased approach, whereby 'key' staff members in certain agencies are trained in its use and

---

88   Available at http://www.dfes.gov.uk/ISA/framework/docs/Draft%20CAF%20Jan%2005.doc

89   EVCM 51, para 8.3.

expected to deploy it; other staff will contact these designated members if they think an assessment needs to be carried out; previously, it has proposed integration of CAF into initial training programmes for professionals, and into Continuing Professional Development; and the production of centrally produced training materials which will be 'cascaded' downwards to the front line. Decisions about who shall receive training initially will be made at local level. These steps seem in general to be a rational response to the challenges and concerns identified by practitioners, but also give rise to questions of their own: Will, for example, the selection of only some staff for training mean that CAF will only be used with a small proportion of children who could have additional needs? Will local authorities find sufficient funds to train staff? How exactly will CAF become part of initial training programmes?

121. With regard to reducing pressures on workload, it is explained that CAF will ultimately lead to a rationalisation of existing assessments and thus reduce the amount of time spent on this activity. It is also proposed that research (discussed in more detail below) will be undertaken to examine the implications of CAF for staff in a variety of settings and that the findings will be used to inform implementation. The rationalisation of assessment through CAF again strikes us as an aspiration rather than a likelihood at this stage, and we will therefore look forward to the results of the research.

Link between assessment and assistance

122. Responses to the DfES consultation raised concerns about the issue of how and whether being assessed through CAF would trigger the provision of services. Some respondents argued that:

> "practitioners would have to be very careful about raising expectations of families by engaging them in the process of a common assessment only to find the needs identified cannot be met, or met within a relatively quick timescale. It was felt this experience could deter families, YP [young people] and children from engaging in the process and would undermine the trust in both the process and public or other services."[90]

123. This seems to us a crucial point, which has also been raised with us in relation to our inquiry. The Refugee Children's Consortium, for example, state that "Assessments should result in action, and the action assessed as needed should be recorded."[91] We would concur that achievement of the aims of CAF are only likely to be attained if there are sufficient resources in the system to actually provide the services for the need(s) identified.

124. Groups representing parents have pointed out that it is sometimes very difficult currently for parents to obtain access to the assessment that they need to 'trigger' assistance for their children. Currently, they argue, the withholding of assessment can be a gate-keeping measure employed by hard-stretched service providers, who have no other choice

90 Department for Education and Skills, *Common Assessment Framework. Analysis of responses to the consultation document*, 2005, available from http://www.dfes.gov.uk/ISA/framework/docs/CAF%20consultation%20-%20full%20report.doc

91 EVCM 38, para 4.13.

but to limit access to services in some way[92]. In its response to the consultation, the DfES indicated that:

> "The decision to undertake an assessment in any individual case will be a matter for professional judgement in light of local practice. It is *not* intended that a CAF must be completed before services can be delivered, or to lay down a blanket threshold at which a common assessment must always be completed."[93]

This stance has been maintained in the draft guidance. While this is in keeping with the strong presumption toward devolved decision-making running throughout *Every Child Matters*, it remains to be seen whether devolving responsibility again to the front line on the issue of when and where the Common Assessment Framework should be used will be a productive way forward.

125. The DfES makes the following comments on how it is intending to progress:

> "We will now look in detail at how the CAF will operate in each of a range of settings (including in schools, health, social services, Connexions, YOTs [youth offending teams] and the police) and in relation to children with specific needs (eg SEN or child protection). We will test the CAF in a number of local areas in 2005-6. And we will carry out assessments of the impact of CAF on specific services before rolling-out CAF nationally."[94]

126. It is essential that the design and implementation of the Common Assessment Framework takes place at a pace that allows informed development. The commitment to further testing and assessment before national rollout is therefore extremely welcome. While it is sensible that the assessments will examine the impacts of Common Assessment Framework on services, we would also hope that they take a broader view and examine the extent to which the Common Assessment Framework is leading to improved outcomes for children, young people and families.

---

92   See for example Q 280.

93   Department for Education and Skills, *DfES response to the consultation report on the Common Assessment Framework*, 2005, available at http://www.dfes.gov.uk/ISA/framework/docs/DfES%20Response%20-%20CAF%20consultation.doc

94   Department for Education and Skills, *DfES response to the consultation report on the Common Assessment Framework*, 2005

7 Integrated strategy and governance

Pacing change

127. The Government has set out a series of demanding milestones and targets that will need to be met by local authorities and others between now and 2008 for the successful implementation of *Every Child Matters*. These include the expectation that most local areas will have Children's Trust arrangements in place by 2006 and that all will have them by 2008. Setting a challenging pace is entirely laudable, but there is an awareness at the front line that rapid change could produce unintended negative consequences. The Local Government Association told the Committee that that one of the potential 'elephant traps' they foresaw was that "people would move too fast and be too enthusiastic about [...] change, and [would] then fall over themselves."[95]

128. This is still clearly an issue that resonates with local strategic bodies, as is evidenced by the response of the Association of Directors of Education and Children's Services and partners to a recent Government consultation on statutory guidance on the implementation of the reforms:

> "we think it [statutory guidance] should reinforce the need for authorities to achieve necessary changes at a pace that suits local circumstances and which places an emphasis on maintaining performance generally and particularly with regard to safeguarding. We are anxious that the guidance may kick-start a rush of changes within authorities which may not be properly prepared nor mirrored, as will be necessary, among relevant and other partners in the area. The guidance should make clear statements about the need for authorities to introduce change in a measured way which suits local circumstance and which promotes rather than jeopardises improvements to children's services."[96]

129. In their oral evidence, the Association of Directors of Social Services were explicit about the specific risks to the most vulnerable children which might follow from 'rushed' implementation:

> "there is a set of issues around the fragility of safeguarding services for child protection concerns, and our concern would obviously be that the majority of authorities which are committed to this arena will work gainfully to protect their children, but there are inevitably going to be children who will slip through the net, and we have to give this agenda time to work forward, and support those authorities that may be struggling with their local competing forces."[97]

130. Our visit to British Columbia in January 2005 further alerted us to the need to ensure change takes place at a reasonable pace. There, we spoke with officials who had observed

---

95 Q 173

96 ADECS, ADSS, Barnardos, Connaught Group, LGA, NCB, NHS Confederation, NSPCC, Children's Society and the Royal College of Pediatrics and Child Health, *Joint response to 'Consultation on draft statutory guidance on the role and responsibilities of the Director for Children's Services and Lead Member for Children's Services'*,2005. The ADSS has recently argued that the draft statutory guidance on Children's Trusts should emphasise that structural change is not a necessity—and that a focus on structure could detract from provision of front line services during transition.

97 Q 166

the implementation of a similarly ambitious programme of reform of children's services and had concluded that driving through change too quickly had had unintended consequences for front line operations. At the front line, there had been a marked shift toward the privileging of safeguarding activities over the delivery of universal services. This had led to professionals becoming risk-averse and consequently taking children into protective custody with increasing frequency.

131. **The Government has made a welcome commitment to respecting local needs, and putting control over change in local hands and we would encourage them to maintain this commitment. Statutory guidance should contain explicit reference to the need to protect front line services during transition, and to implement change at a pace suited to local needs. At the national level the Government can assist by remaining alert for any evidence that unintended negative side-effects of change are occurring, and, especially, that any decrease in the effectiveness of critical front line and child protection services is taking place.**

Integrated inspection arrangements

132. The Government envisages a central role for inspection in the implementation of *Every Child Matters*, with new 'integrated' inspection arrangements to be developed, enabling judgements to be made about the extent to which children in any one area attain the five 'outcomes' underlying the policy proposals. Crucially, integrated inspection will also provide a picture of the way in which services contribute to improving these outcomes through partnership working.

133. Ofsted was asked by the DfES to take the lead on developing proposals for the integrated inspection arrangements, working in partnership with nine other relevant inspectorates.[98] In December 2004, Ofsted released the Framework for Inspection of Children's Services for formal consultation. The Framework has been published alongside several other documents including: *Joint Area Review of Children's Services; Annual Performance Assessment of Council Children's Services; Inspection of Children's Services: Key Judgements and Evidence.* The responses to the consultation are due to be published in February 2005 and the Framework for Inspection must be issued finally, in accordance with statute, in May 2005. Key proposals include:

- An overarching 'Framework' for the inspection of children's services, which will influence the focus of institutional inspections carried out by all relevant inspectorates.

- From 2005, combined Annual Performance Assessment (by Ofsted and the Commission for Social Care Inspection) of council education and social care services for children and young people.

- Joint Area Reviews which will assess the experience of children and young people and report on outcomes for them. They will evaluate the contributions made by a wide range of services and the way these services work together to improve outcomes. JARs will be conducted at the same time as CPA corporate assessment.

---

98 Commission for Social Care Inspection, Probation Inspectorate, Audit Commission, Magistrates' Courts Service Inspectorate, Prisons Inspectorate, Constabulary Inspectorate, Adult Learning Inspectorate, Healthcare Commission, HM Crown Prosecution Service Inspectorate.

- Consultation of children, young people and parents during inspections.[99]

134. We have been very impressed at the progress that has been made with regard to the planning of integrated inspection over the last year. The timetable set out by the Government for the development of proposals was demanding, with a statutory requirement for the framework for inspection of children's services to be issued finally by May 2005 and the expectation that integrated inspection arrangements will begin to be implemented in September 2005. Ofsted and partners have responded well to this, taking a consultative approach which has been praised in some of the evidence we have received. They have also stayed close to the outcomes-oriented approach taken in the proposals as a whole.

135. Since we took evidence, it has been announced that the Commission for Social Care Inspection (CSCI) is to be disbanded, with its children and young people's functions being subsumed into Ofsted[100]. Arguably this will make integrated inspection more achievable, although the Committee was already impressed by the evidence of joint working between the CSCI and Ofsted. It will be important that the subsuming of the CSCI into Ofsted does not lead to any devaluation of the significance of the social care perspective and experience. We will be watching developments closely in this area.

136. It is difficult to forecast the likely success of the new inspection regime as final arrangements have not yet been confirmed. There are nevertheless a number of specific issues about which we have some initial concerns including: whether the proposed arrangements are likely to provide a satisfactory measure of attainment of the five outcomes; lack of clarity about the consequences of failed inspections—and more generally, the role of inspection in the improvement cycle; likely effectiveness of arrangements to involve children and young people in inspections; training needs of joint inspection teams; and the ability of Ofsted to serve as lead agency while at the same time experiencing significant personnel cuts and restructuring. These are addressed in turn below.

Accurately measuring attainment of outcomes

137. Joint Area Reviews will seek to provide an objective analysis of outcomes for children in a local area, as well as looking at the extent to which individual services contribute to those outcomes through partnership working. The five outcomes each now have attached five associated 'aims.'[101] In terms of inspection, the 25 aims provide a more detailed set of criteria against which progress can be measured.

138. Commenting generally on the definition of outcomes in the original Green Paper, Prof. Peter Moss noted:

"Targets and outcomes can be treated as purely managerial tools, without appreciating that these are necessarily contestable in a democratic and pluralist society because they raise important ethical and political questions. For example,

99   See http://www.ofsted.gov.uk/childrenandyoungpeople/

100   This was announced in Budget 2005: HM Treasury, *Budget 2005*, Ch. 6.23, pp. 142, 2005

101   See Appendix A.

why is the outcome 'being healthy' described [...] in terms of avoiding negative behaviours? Or why is 'enjoying and achieving' reduced to school achievement?"[102]

139. The relative success of inspections of children's services will depend to some extent on whether the 25 associated 'aims' truly reflect the meaning of the five parent 'outcomes' and whether, in turn, the evidence that is relied upon to gauge progress toward the outcomes and aims is appropriate. We appreciate that Ofsted and partners are currently consulting on the suitability of the proposed inspection framework, including the validity of the 25 related aims and the indicators used to measure progress toward them. We look forward to the results of this consultation and may pursue this issue further when the outcomes are known.

Inspection and improvement

140. The connection between inspection and improvement has occupied us as a Committee and is a subject we have previously discussed at length with Her Majesty's Chief Inspector of Schools.[103] **We maintain that for inspection to serve as a lever for improvement, there needs to be a clear process linking inspection findings, communication of these findings to service(s) inspected, and suitable intervention to bring about change.**

141. With regard to the integrated inspection arrangements proposed under *Every Child Matters*, we are not yet clear of how the 'improvement through inspection' process will work in practice. In oral evidence, the Minister told us:

"We [...] have pretty tough performance assessment, both from our regional advisors, from the inspectors, and we have the joint area review at local level, which is all the inspectors coming together to see how well an area is delivering services for children. All that gives us the framework to measure performance, and star ratings and all that stuff flows from it. If authorities fail children through the services they provide, we will intervene. We have a new power under the Children Act which mirrors the power of intervention into local education authorities and we will intervene"[104]

142. We welcome this statement by the Minister but we are not clear as to the specific procedures which will be triggered should Joint Area Review find local services lacking or failing to improve.

143. **To play the critical role in *Every Child Matters* that the Government envisages, integrated inspection must ultimately contribute to the improvement of services. We would welcome clarification on how this will happen with regard to inspections of children's services. The specific procedures which will be triggered should a local area be deemed by integrated inspection to be failing require clearer explanation. In particular, it needs to be made clear how the findings of area reviews will be played back**

102 EVCM 16, para 17.

103 See, for example, Education and Skills Committee, *The work of Ofsted*, HC 426, 2004.

104 Q 500

to individual service providers, and how these will be used to bring about improvement.

Integrated inspection teams and joint training

144. The integrated inspection arrangements propose that teams of inspectors will conduct joint fieldwork – teams could include, therefore, employees of Ofsted, the Commission for Social Care Inspection (CSCI)[105] and the Healthcare Commission, among others. This poses some challenges for inspectorates who have traditionally employed different methodologies and approaches. Her Majesty's Chief Inspector recognised this when giving evidence to the Committee on an earlier occasion:

> "The Social Services Inspectorate as was—the CSCI as is now—has a history of looking at individual case files as part of its work with local authorities. One of the very interesting questions that we have been debating with the CSCI is how you, in doing children's services inspections, capture the big picture at the same time as focussing down on those individual case files. Interestingly that will be a feature and will continue to be a feature of inspection with CSI so when we are doing children's services inspections they will be exactly what you have described. The problem with that, of course, is—and this has been very interesting for Ofsted because this has not been part of our methodology in the past—how many case files do you look at to get the picture?"[106]

145. We asked Ofsted and partners about their plans to jointly train inspectors. We were pleased to hear that groups of inspectors from different inspectorates had already been meeting and that they would be "brought together more extensively after Christmas, to start training programmes together".[107] Further details from Ofsted and partners on the scale and nature of joint training for inspectors would be welcome, and we will also be interested to hear from them over the coming period what progress is being made in this regard.

Ofsted's role as lead agency at a time of restructuring

146. Like other Government departments, Ofsted are committed to making significant personnel cuts and efficiency savings over the coming period. We have considered whether this might have implications for their ability to act as the lead agency in the design and implementation of integrated inspections of children's services. The Public and Commercial Services Union was recently quoted in the press as saying that that the proposed reorganisation of, and cuts in, Ofsted's staffing would 'compromise the safety of children'[108]. In oral evidence, Her Majesty's Chief Inspector strongly contested assertions that cuts would undermine Ofsted's ability to deliver. Restructuring, he contended, was

---

105 As discussed in paragraph 134, the CSCI and Ofsted will eventually be merged.

106 Q 67

107 Q 94

108 "Ofsted cuts put children in danger, warn unions," *The Guardian*, Wed 24th November, 2004.
     http://society.guardian.co.uk/children/story/0,1074,1358178,00.html

necessary and would not affect the ability of the organisation to discharge its responsibilities, even at a time where its general remit is widening significantly.[109]

147. We appreciate the considerable efforts which have gone into developing a 'unified and efficient approach' to inspection, and accept that in principle this confers the potential for joint inspections to be less of an 'additional burden' for both inspectorates and services than might otherwise have been the case. Joint Area Reviews, for example, will replace or subsume inspection of area 14-19 provision, Local Education Authorities and inspections of Connexions services—all currently conducted by Ofsted. Additionally, they will also make use of data from existing inspections. However, Joint Area Reviews will still demand resources from Ofsted and other inspectorates. They will use a wide range of strategies for gathering evidence including case studies, neighbourhood studies[110] and interviews with children and young people.

148. On balance, we feel that the Public and Commercial Services Union's assessment is, at this stage, unduly pessimistic. In our report on the *Work of Ofsted 2004,*[111] we concluded that it was likely that the organisation would be able to meet both existing and new responsibilities, including those associated with *Every Child Matters,* and we see no case for arriving at a different judgement here. Ongoing scrutiny of Ofsted is a part of our remit as a Committee, and we will remain attentive for any signs that cuts are undermining the effectiveness of their leadership role in children's services inspections or their capacity to effectively participate in joint area inspections.

Local co-operation arrangements: involving schools and GPs

149. Individual schools and General Practitioners are not placed under a duty to co-operate in local Children's Trust arrangements by the Children Act 2004. Several groups argued during the passage of the Act for an amendment to achieve this aim, but the argument was rejected by the Government primarily on the grounds that the duty to collaborate should be at 'strategic level'. As it stands, Primary Care Trusts and Local Authorities are required to co-operate in Children's Trusts and it is argued that these will be the main means for drawing GPs and schools respectively into joint planning, commissioning and delivery arrangements. Additionally, the Government has said that it intends to make clear through statutory guidance and other means that schools and GPs (as well as other agencies not included in the duty to co-operate) will be expected to participate where appropriate.

150. However, witnesses repeatedly told us that they fear that a minority of schools and some GPs may not participate fully in local co-operation arrangements in the absence of a statutory duty to do so. **We are not convinced that the levers for participation suggested by the Government will provide the necessary safeguards. This is especially true in the light of policy tensions in the DfES, which appear to be producing contradictory drivers and to be demanding conflicting responses from schools and service providers.**

---

109 Q 139

110 Although it is proposed that, as a rule, new fieldwork will only be undertaken when other suitable alternative data sources cannot be found.

111 ibid

Every Child Matters 47

151. One such tension is particularly apparent when the *Five Year Strategy for Children and Learners*[112] and *Every Child Matters* are considered side by side. The former advances policies which give schools more independence and autonomy—for example, through the easier attainment of Foundation status. The *Five Year Strategy* also fundamentally alters schools' relationships with Local authorities – increasingly, money is being given direct to schools, usurping the traditional role of authorities as strategic bodies and providers of funds.

152. *Every Child Matters*, on the other hand, envisages local partnerships between groups of schools and/or schools and other local services. The former policy strand clearly has implications for the success of the latter, as David Bell recognised:

> "there is no hiding from the fact that schools do have a high degree of autonomy and may choose, for whatever reason, not to cooperate or to collaborate in the same sort of way with other schools or the local services more generally. That is the way in which we have constructed policy, and I think we have to recognise that that is there and trust—and I think it is not just a finger in the wind, it is a real expectation—that schools will see the virtues of cooperation and collaboration with other services for the sake of the children in their care."[113]

The LGA are, however, somewhat more circumspect about how things are likely to work in practice:

> "Whilst I think no-one has a problem with school autonomy as it stands at the moment, there is a concern about relying on the goodwill and spirit of individuals to see that the duty to collaborate is a kind of moral imperative as opposed to a legalistic duty that is being placed on everybody else."[114]

153. In February 2005, the Association of Directors of Education and Children's Services, Confederation of Education Services Managers (ConfED), National Association of Head Teachers, National Association of School Governors, National Governors Council, Secondary Heads Association and the Advisory Centre for Education issued a joint statement in response to the DfES policy toward independent specialist schools as laid out in the *Five Year Strategy for Children and Learners*. This statement argues forcefully that the increasing independence of schools may be incompatible with other policies steering schools toward local co-operation. They stated:

> "We believe that school autonomy should be in a framework of collaboration and we are concerned that the emphasis on 'independence' in the Five Year Strategy is not balanced by sufficiently strong measures to encourage schools to work together. In our experience, few schools want actively to compete at the expense of neighbouring schools and very few, if any, schools will refuse to co-operate. Excellence in Cities partnerships are a good example of active collaboration, even between schools that had hitherto been in strong competition. We expect the guidance to schools under

112 .Department for Education and Skills,*Five Year Strategy for Children and Learners*, CM 6272, July 2004.

113 Q 109

114 Q 159

the Children Act 2004 to emphasise the importance of such collaboration, and we look to the Government to provide appropriate incentives for them to do so."[115]

154. The evidence that we have taken in the course of other inquiries has convinced us that encouragement and exhortation to schools to change their practice is not always sufficient to secure commitment to policy proposals. In our inquiry into school admissions[116], we found ample evidence that some schools were choosing to ignore the advisory admissions code, and we therefore recommended that the code be given statutory status. Disappointingly, the Government rejected our recommendation.

155. We are therefore deeply concerned that a similar voluntaristic approach is being pursued with regard to schools' participation in the local co-operation arrangements expected as part of *Every Child Matters*, when there is demonstrable evidence that schools do not always perceive the standards and inclusion agendas as being complementary – and consequently will occasionally act in ways that 'raise' standards and preserve autonomy at the expense of inclusion and local co-operation.

156. The Government has consistently argued that schools will be encouraged to engage with the *Every Child Matters* agenda through the lever of inspection. Consequently, the current Education Bill will place a new duty on Ofsted to inspect schools on:

- how far the education provided in the school meets the needs of the range of pupils at the school;

- the contribution made by the school to the wellbeing of those pupils.

However, this does not necessarily imply that schools will be inspected specifically on the extent to which they co-operate with other schools and agencies in their area.

157. Partnership working by all local services (including schools and GPs) *will* be assessed as part of Joint Area Reviews, but, as we made clear in the section on integrated inspection above, it is currently somewhat unclear how area findings will be related back to individual services – and how consequently Joint Area Reviews will contribute to improvement.

158. The Royal College of General Practitioners sees a solution in linking inspection findings directly with funding allocations:

"There needs to be penalties associated with failure as, in this way, health, social services and education can be reasonably expected to prioritise many of the currently unfunded issues unless mechanisms are introduced, including inspection, which makes it clear that resources will be under threat unless demonstrable progress and appropriate quality standards are being applied at a local level."[117].

159. We are not currently aware of any plans to link funding allocations to inspection outcomes in the case of schools, and there are many reasons why such an avenue might not be considered constructive or workable. However, the Royal College's comments do point

115 ADECS *et.al. School Autonomy and Accountability; a Joint Statement,* February 2004.

116 Education and Skills Committee, Fourth Report of Session 2003–04, *Secondary Education: School Admissions,* HC 58–
  I.

117 EVCM 22, para 12.

to the need for further reassurance that inspection arrangements will function as a sufficiently powerful lever to ensure full participation.

160. As regards securing the full involvement of GPs in local partnership arrangements, the NHS Confederation told us:

> "Primary care trusts regard it as a challenge to engage all GPs, and they are very keen to see some proper incentives in the system to enable them to do that [...] It will also have to happen through things like re-validation and through the quality and outcomes framework, because we know those are things that doctors inter-relate with quite intimately, because at the end of the day they affect pay; and something which affects pay is more likely to be a powerful driver of conformity than something that is enshrined in statute. We have some mechanisms for making sure that it does not become a problem around GPs, which are potentially easier to deal with than some of the concerns around schools."[118.]

161. We are pleased to hear that practical and creative methods for securing the engagement of GPs in local co-operation arrangements are being tabled, and we think that this is something that the Government could usefully pursue with the relevant agencies. We can see the logic, reiterated to us by both the Minister and the Secretary of State, in placing a legal duty to cooperate upon strategic bodies rather than operational agencies. The rationale behind this presumably relates to the 'purchaser-provider split', with the assumption that funds lie with the strategic bodies, which, by coordinating their approach, can require cooperation from provider agencies. However, this does not seem to apply in the case of schools and GPs. The policy intention in both cases is to locate funding at the front line—with schools rather than Local Authorities, and GP practices rather than Primary Care Trusts, thereby diminishing the commissioning power of strategic agencies. We are accordingly concerned that the absence upon schools and GPs of a duty to cooperate could seriously undermine the development of local 'whole systems' approaches.

162. **We await final confirmation of the details of integrated inspection, but we are deeply concerned that some schools, GPs and other services not under a statutory duty to collaborate in Children's Trust agreements may choose, for one reason or another, not to participate. This has the potential to fundamentally undermine the aims and intentions of Every Child Matters. It is unlikely that the current incentives and penalties in the system will be adequate to make reluctant schools, in particular, co-operate. The Government needs to clarify what additional incentives will be introduced into the system to address this issue, and especially, what changes will be made to the framework for the inspection of schools.**

163. It is vital that the contribution of the voluntary and community sector is not overlooked or diminished. This is a complex sector, including big national charities on the one hand and very small community-based organisations on the other. This can lead to difficulties in engaging the sector with strategic planning and commissioning processes[119]. There is also concern within the sector about local mainstreaming of the Children's Fund and Sure Start local programmes, both areas in which voluntary and community bodies

118 Q 161

119 On this issue, see Kendall, J. *The Voluntary Sector: comparative perspectives in the UK,*2003, London: Routledge.

have played a large part. **We will be following closely the effect of the *Every Child Matters* changes on the voluntary and community sector and hope that the large and valuable contribution it makes will be recognised and sustained.**

Joint commissioning and budget-pooling

164. The Government intends that budget-pooling will increasingly occur between service providers to enable the joint commissioning of services. While this is not compulsory, the Government contends that it will be a "very, very powerful tool"[120] for providing more joined-up and responsive services. There is much support for the aims of shared financial responsibility and joint commissioning of services. Contact a Family argued:

> "The principles behind Children's Trusts are sound. Parents speak to us about their frustration in having to repeat the same information time and again to different departments and then being passed from one to the other while financial responsibility is argued out. Pooled budgets across the LEA, Children's Social Services and health services must be a positive step forward in alleviating many of these problems."[121]

165. On the other hand, some witnesses sounded a note of caution about budget-pooling in particular. While this is often an admirable aim, the process of implementation needs careful thought. The Association of Directors of Education and Children's Services told us:

> "We would like to see some progress on pooling of budgets, but only when it is clear what the budgets are that we are pooling, what we are pooling them for and what the service specification is for pooling them. There have been some examples of pooled budgets before their time, which have not resulted in any service improvements. We would argue that the service specification, the review of the services—what James was saying in terms of looking at the middle part of that triangle, targeted services for children in need, needs to be got right; then you look at how you will pool the budgets to get the service into the shape you really wanted to serve the children better. This is a massive programme of change. It is clear that local authorities and their partners up and down the country are at very different stages in that process."[122]

166. This sentiment was echoed in written evidence submitted by the Audit Commission, which argued:

> "The experience of many local authorities and NHS bodies, as well as our own experience as auditors, has shown that pooling budgets often poses a range of challenges that can be extremely time consuming to resolve. Partners need to be very clear about the added value of budget pooling, and their individual and joint commitment to the work before taking this route."[123]

167. The Association of Directors of Social Services further reinforced this point:

120   Q 405

121   EVCM 8, section 4.

122   Q 172

123   EVCM 49, para 2.2.

"[regarding VAT and budgetary cycles]... I think they are serious obstacles. Some of the bureaucracy around pooling budgets is part of the disincentive, and the work that is required to get through that bureaucracy, we certainly feel in the smaller authority, can be better invested in developing some of the cultural arrangements about joint working and look again [...] about what were the outcomes that we were intending from the pool. We would enter into it very hesitantly, particularly around services. We can find very easy ways of making sure the shared money is getting to the service user without getting into complex bureaucratic arrangements which are not necessarily going to help, and I think the evidence-base for them is a bit weak."[124]

168. While the evidence we have seen has convinced us that joint commissioning of services is a laudable and worthwhile aim that can offer significant benefits for children and young people in terms of the services they receive, we think a more cautious approach needs to be pursued in relation to across-the-board budget pooling by Children's Trusts. We understand that the evidence from evaluations of the section 31 arrangements under the Health Act 1999 suggests that pooled budgets only add value where there is already a high degree of trust and clarity of purpose amongst the partners.[125] Pooled budgets are therefore best thought of as one more tool in the partnership armoury, rather than an accounting panacea. It will be important to assess progress in this respect, and it is disappointing that the Minister has told us in supplementary evidence that the DfES does not even propose to collect information about the budgets that will be pooled through the Children's Trusts.[126]

169. **Statutory guidance and other communications which concern themselves with budget-pooling need to make absolutely clear that local areas should not pursue such pooling for its own sake. Until sufficient evidence has been amassed from Pathfinder Children's Trusts on best practice in this area, it would be preferable to give a clear steer for local areas to thoroughly analyse the benefits likely to accrue from budget-pooling before embarking on the process.**

Director of Children's Services

170. It is now a statutory requirement for each top-tier Local Authority to appoint a Director of Children's Services (DCS) and Lead (council) Member. It is intended that the DCS will provide strategic leadership for Children's Trusts as well as being an accountable figurehead. The DfES is currently consulting on the statutory guidance for the Directors of Children's Services and Lead Member roles.

Background of appointees

171. By March 2005, approximately 50% of Local Authorities had made Directors of Children's Services appointments, around 90% of whom had previously been Directors of Education[127]. With relatively few appointees from a social care background, some have

---

124 Q 192

125 Hudson, B. et. al., *National Evaluation of Notifications of Use of the Section 31 Partnership Flexibilities of the Health Act 1999*, 2002, Nuffield Institute for Health/National Primary Care Research & Development Centre.

126 EVCM 74.

127 Qq 383–385

argued that this amounts to an 'educational takeover' of the new integrated children's services.

172. The skills profile has also raised some concerns about whether the Directors of Children's Services are likely to have the requisite level of professional knowledge: if experienced directors of social services are, in the main, not being appointed to DCS roles, it has to be a concern that expertise on crucial issues such as child protection may not be immediately apparent at directorial level. The Commission for Social Care Inspection commented:

> "It is essential that the range of skills which the new Directors of Children's Service possess, draw together the experiences of both Directors of Education and Directors of Social Services. It is essential that there is no loss of expertise and knowledge of children's social care. The Commission will be working closely with local councils to ensure that social care services for children are not seen as an add on to some reorganised education department, and that health services, the police and the youth justice system are kept as inclusive components of the development of children's services. Children's Services Directorates are not simply education departments by another name."[128]

173. The DfES, in response, told us that they would not be seeking to direct local areas in the kinds of appointments they made, as that would be inappropriate. They also told us that, in their view, what was important was the general managerial and strategic competency possessed by appointees to the DCS roles. While we understand that the DfES cannot interfere in the appointment process we do feel on balance that this is an area that could benefit from closer monitoring, as the appointments process gathers pace.

Responsibility without power?

174. Children's Services Authorities will be judged, through inspection, on the effectiveness of services as a whole in their area. Directors of Children's Services, as figureheads, will therefore bear a large degree of responsibility and accountability for outcomes for children in their area. The Association of Directors of Education and Children's Services and partners pointed to an interesting and potentially problematic anomaly in relation to the discharge of the DCS' duty. While, managerially, he or she will be responsible for the Local Authority only, the scope of the role in reality goes much further. This, they contend, is likely to raise a number of operational problems:

> "There is no indication of what powers if any the DCS has if partners do not fulfil their various statutory responsibilities in a satisfactory way, thus undermining the partnership arrangements. This section should make more explicit reference to how the DCS can hold partners to account and where necessary alert the relevant internal authority or inspectorate."[129]

175. Speaking on behalf of the LGA, Cllr. James Kempton told us:

---

128 EVCM 60, para 4.2.

129 Response to *Consultation on Draft Statutory Guidance on the Role and Responsibilities of the Director of Children's Services and Lead Member for Children's Services*, ADECS et.al, 2005.

"I think local authorities would say that they have some anxieties about the assessment of their performance through corporate performance assessment, for example, against the performance effectively of other authorities with whom they have the ability to influence but not necessarily the ability to control. The issue of accountability of that authority is one of concern to us [...] we are used to working with a whole range of partners, and we are used to working in an area of accountability without authority, but that does not mean to say that that is necessarily the preferable place to be."[130]

He went on to add that there were potentially other avenues for holding partners to account—through, for example, performance assessment and inspection. However, the issue of authority without power seems to us to indicate a fundamental problem, and one which it would not be entirely appropriate to expect Directors of Children's Services themselves to resolve.

176. **The DfES is currently consulting on the Director of Children's Services role. When statutory guidance is finally issued, it must make explicit the actions which will be open to Directors of Children's Services should essential partners fail to co-operate.**

Children's Trust boards and Local Safeguarding Children Boards

177. The DfES has stressed that the successful establishment and operation of Children's Trusts will require local areas to develop and implement strong proposals for shared governance, partly to "hold [...] things together through tough times as well as good".[131] As in other areas, the DfES has stressed that decisions about the exact arrangements for governance of local partnership arrangements will be made at the local level, although it is intended that decision-making on this crucial issue will be guided by "learning and research on interagency governance and accountability through the Children's Trust pathfinders."[132]

178. We agree with the Audit Commission's analysis of the potential benefits and risks of such an approach:

"The lack of specificity on governance arrangements for children's trusts reflects an opportunity to accommodate local circumstances but does carry with it risks associated with a variation of approach, practices, systems, participation, competences and accountabilities."[133]

179. Our evidence raises a number of questions and concerns about specific aspects of governance arrangements. One particular issue is the lack of clarity surrounding the relationship between Local Safeguarding Children Boards and Children's Trust boards. The LGA told us they had:

---

130 Q 187

131 Q 407

132 Department for Education and Skills, *Every Child Matters: Change for Children*, para 3.49, p 23.

133 EVCM 49, para 17.

"concerns about the lack of clarity between the duty to collaborate and the duty to set up Local Safeguarding Boards. There is a lack of co-terminosity [...] between the two and with different relationships regarding accountability and governance. It's feasible that the co-operation arrangements for example through the strategic partnership, and the LSCB could act independently of each other."[134]

180. Another area of concern is how boards will relate back to the executive bodies of their respective member organisations. TEN, the Democratic Health Network and the Local Government Information Unit argued in their joint submission:

"We have concerns over arrangements for ensuring accountability and transparency for Trust decisions through its member organisations. The substantial differences between governance arrangements of democratically accountable local authorities and Primary Care Trusts, as well as differences in culture and priorities, will pose considerable challenges for Chairs of Trusts or partnerships. All this raises the question of how do Trusts link back to the executive bodies of the local authority and other partners?"[135]

The Audit Commission made a very similar point:

"The governance arrangements for each sector are different. Local government and health agencies are accountable to different bodies, one democratically elected, the other not, which can pose challenges in terms of accountability and perceived legitimacy in relation to joint working. In addition, health and education are both delivered by independent practitioners (GPs) and organisations (schools). Either of these may legitimately work to different objectives to those of local authorities and Primary Care Trusts, introducing additional challenges to coordination and to a common accountability framework."[136]

181. The crucial issue of governance of Children's Trust arrangements is another example of the potential risks and benefits of a locally led approach to development. Given the importance of good governance to the successful implementation of Children's Trust arrangements, we think that in this instance there is a strong case for clearer guidance from a central source. The commitment, made in *Change for Children*, to mainstreaming the knowledge acquired from Children's Trust pathfinders on this issue is welcome, although as elsewhere we note that Pathfinder development (and analysis of that development) is still at a relatively early stage and therefore its ability to inform is more limited than is desirable.

182. Children's Trusts will also have the key role to play in developing the Children and Young People's Partnership Plans (CYPPP) required under section 17 of the 2004 Children Act, and upon which guidance is due later this year. The expectation is that the CYPPPs will be aligned with other local strategic plans, including the NHS Local Delivery Plan and the Youth Justice Plan, with the Local Strategic Partnership then forming an overarching view of local needs and strategies in the Community Plan. There is therefore an additional

---

134 EVCM 51, para 3.6

135 EVCM 17, pap 3.3

136 EVCM 49, para 15

governance issue, yet to be addressed, concerned with the relationship between the Children's Trusts and Local Strategic Partnerships.

8 Inter-departmental and Governmental issues

Funding—overall costs of programme of reform

183. *Every Child Matters* is an extremely ambitious and expensive programme. However, a transparent summary of the extra resources that have been allocated centrally by the Government for implementation is difficult to obtain. When we asked the Minister if she could provide a breakdown of the funding allotted to *Every Child Matters* as a whole, she referred us[137] to the breakdown contained in the document *Every Child Matters; Change for Children,* which is as follows:

- In 2004–05 and in 2005–06 all Local Authorities are receiving a Safeguarding Children Grant of £90 million

- A Change Fund grant of £15 million, for an 18-month period to March 2006, allocated across all Local Authorities to help them to build on progress in setting in place children's trust arrangements.

- Grant resources for ongoing work to reduce teenage pregnancy, improve the life chances of looked after children, including through improving foster care and increasing adoption and special guardianship, for improving child and adolescent mental health services, and for supporting the development of extended schools.

- The Government will be making available £22.5 million in 2006–07 and £63 million in 2007–08 to help Local Authorities to implement the changes in *Every Child Matters: Change for Children.*

- £15 million in 2006-2007 and £30 million in 2007-2008 for the Children's Workforce Development Council to deliver the workforce reform agenda.

- £500 million rise in the Formula Spending Share for children's social services between 2005–06 and 2007–08 to a total of £4.5 billion; increase of £769 million between 2004–05 and 2007–08 in early years and childcare.

- Children's health services will also benefit from growth in NHS expenditure by almost 70% in six years from £33 billion to almost £56 billion. It will rise steadily over the next five years to more than £90 billion.

- A further £1 million in 2006–07 and £2 million in 2007–08 to support voluntary and community organisations to engage with local change, as set out in 'Working with voluntary and community organisations to deliver change for children and young people.[138]

---

137 EVCM 74

138 Adapted from *Every Child Matters: Change for Children.*

184. It has repeatedly been made clear that local change programmes will be funded in the main through the better use of existing resources rather than through additional dedicated money. The Minister for Children told us that:

> "If we are even half successful in our ambition to transform the way people work, we do not necessarily need more money; we simply really do need to use existing resources more smartly."[139]

The introduction to the financial breakdown outlined above also makes this very clear:

> "There are already significant resources devoted to improving outcomes for children and young people in Local Authorities, local health services and other partners such as Connexions, Youth Offending Teams and Children's Fund partnerships. Many of the activities underway will, as well as leading to better outcomes, improve efficiency by removing duplication between services and bringing budgets together where appropriate."[140]

185. The Government argues that a programme which identifies and tackles problems early will in the long term lead to fewer children and young people needing costly interventions at a later stage in life, and ultimately placing fewer demands on the welfare state. It also contends—as in the passage above—that better integrated services will reduce duplication and overlap and therefore save resources. We can see the logic in these arguments. Dr. Deborah Ghate, Director of the Policy Research Bureau and author of a recent review of international research evidence on parenting support told us:

> "the point about the argument on cost is yes, all these reforms will be very expensive if they do not work but if they do work they will be tremendously cost effective because the costs of poor outcomes for children in the long term, both social outcomes and in terms of cost to the Exchequer, are enormous, and we know from the relatively few cost effectiveness studies that have been done on some of the interventions to deal with children at greatest risk that when they work they save money. It is about taking the long view."[141]

186. The necessity of providing expensive 'fire fighting' interventions to address acute problems has in the past led to a situation where there are few resources left over to invest in preventative services—as the Government has rightly identified. However, even if we accept that better universal and preventative services are likely to be cost-effective in the long term, we would still contend that in the short- to medium- term additional investment is likely to be required to improve and expand preventative services for *all* children while concurrently maintaining or improving targeted services for those with acute needs. **We think—and our concern is amplified by what witnesses have told us – that the additional resources needed to 'bridge' the transition from 'fire fighting' to more effective preventive, universally accessible services are unlikely to be found through 'efficiency savings' generated by services working in a more 'joined-up' way**[142].

---

139 Q 496

140 ibid, pp 28.

141 Q 283

142 See for example EVCM 54, para. 28.

Costs of transition and training

187. We are particularly concerned that the costs of transition to the new arrangements are vastly underestimated. The evidence we have received indicates that two areas in particular are likely to be extremely costly in the short- to medium-term: initial training for staff—which we discussed in more detail in section four, above; and the establishment and ongoing administration of Children's Trust arrangements. The 35 pathfinder Children's Trusts were each allotted £60,000–£100,000 pump-priming money to develop their local partnership arrangements. However, we understand from the *Every Child Matters* documentation that a change fund of only £15 million across all Local Authorities has been allotted specifically to help non-Pathfinder local areas develop their Children's Trust arrangements. This amount seems worryingly small and this is especially concerning in the light of initial evidence from the interim evaluation of Children's Trusts, which found that:

> "Pathfinder informants felt that potential efficiency gains could result from children's trusts [...] however, several pathfinders highlighted that a key barrier to children's trust development was difficulty in securing dedicated funding to adequately resource the effective development of integrative arrangements."[143]

188. **The evidence we have seen has not convinced us that the financial implications of the *Every Child Matters* programme of reform have been properly assessed or comprehensively modelled, and it is therefore not clear on what basis the Government is able to assume that *Every Child Matters* will be largely self-financing. We recognise and welcome the significant extra resources for primary school capital projects, announced in Budget 2005 which, it is intended, will be used partly to support the *Every Child Matters* agenda.[144] However, we are still unclear as to whether capital building, adaptation or maintenance costs associated with the roll-out of Extended Schools and Sure Start Children's Centres have been properly modelled.** In the absence of comprehensive modelling, and in the light of what we have been told by witnesses involved in transforming services at the front line, we are forced to conclude that there is a risk that the aims of *Every Child Matters* will fail to be realised without significant and sustained additional investment—particularly for crucial areas such as workforce development and the establishment of Children's Trusts. This is particularly concerning given past precedent—it is widely accepted that failure to implement the Children Act of 1989[145], widely perceived as a solid piece of legislation, has been largely due to a lack of resources.

189. **We are doubtful that a policy as ambitious as *Every Child Matters* can be funded in the main from existing budgets. Better deployment of existing resources is a laudable aim, but we believe the Government needs to lead from the top on this issue and build up an evidence base which demonstrates how this can be achieved in practice.**

190. **Our evidence demonstrates that at the very least, in respect of some specific areas of policy there is a strong case for identifying additional funds for implementation,**

---

143   ibid, para 251.

144   HM Treasury , *Budget 2005*, Ch. 6. 2005.

145   Children Act 1989, C.41.

over and above those which have already been put aside. These areas include, but are not limited to, workforce development and the setup and maintenance of Children's Trusts. The Government should therefore consider committing additional dedicated resources—cross-departmentally and ring-fenced if appropriate—to enable successful implementation of *Every Child Matters.*

DfES restructuring

191. As outlined in its recent *Five Year Strategy for Children and Learners*[146], the DfES is planning to cut staffing levels by 31% by 2008. We discussed with DfES Officials our concerns about how this restructuring might affect the ability of the Children, Young People and Families Directorate (CYPFD) to implement *Every Child Matters.* They confirmed that the directorate would indeed "come down in size alongside and perhaps a little bit more than the departmental average",[147] but argued that they did not foresee this having a negative impact on their ability to drive through reform; they would be "reducing in size but […] seeking to do so in a way which is about supporting change for children".[148]

192. We are not persuaded that this is more than an aspiration – and one that is unlikely to be achieved at that. In our recent report on Public Expenditure[149] we were critical of the way in which departmental restructuring had been approached, and expressed concern about the potential negative effect this might have on the work of the department. Similarly, we are not convinced by the reasoning relied upon to claim that job cuts in the CYPFD are compatible with the demands of implementing *Every Child Matters.*

193. The Children, Young People and Families Directorate told us that rationalisation would lead to the directorate being much more strategic in its approach, and to move away from the micro-management of local services. This involved—in the case of *Every Child Matters*—devolving much of the responsibility for the implementation of *Every Child Matters* to Local Authorities who would be largely responsible for developing Children's Trusts. Additionally, the CYPFD (in common with other directorates) would, they told us, be looking for "a more effective way of working through government offices and we need authoritative respected interlocutors with key people leading change in local areas. We have a lot of work to do around that."[150]

194. The Public and Commercial Services Union (PCSU)—who have members working in the CYPFD—were strongly critical of the proposed changes and argued that they are likely to make successful implementation of *Every Child Matters* unlikely:

> "the DfES' role in the sector is […] already highly strategic while front line responsibilities rest with its partners […] Therefore PCS does not accept that the Organisational Review has created a new role for CYPFD; it remains responsible for overarching policy for services and support for children. The impact of job cuts

146 ibid, ch. 9

147 Q 395

148 Q 394

149 Education and Skills Select Committee, First Report of Session 2004–05, *Public Expenditure on Education and Skills,* HC 168.

150 Q 395

across CYPFD on its capacity to deliver its policy and operational function has been acknowledged by CYPFD in a note to its staff, when it was admitted that *"reducing the size of the Directorate while transforming the service we offer and achieving better outcomes for children and families is a tall order; it will be difficult for all of us at times"* […] Continuing to make staffing reductions across CYPFD in the present circumstances amount, in PCS's view, to the creation of additional and avoidable risks to the success of a major initiative."[151]

195. With regard to proposals to work more effectively with local partners through redeployment of 'field forces' and review of regional staffing arrangements, the PCSU further commented:

"PCS now believes, on the basis of feedback from members, that a further cut of 10 posts, beyond those already announced and implemented, are planned for CYPFD's regional teams in the near future; such a cut could result in the closure of smaller CYPFD regional teams such as those in Plymouth and Liverpool, and will further undermine the DfES's capacity to support front line practitioners at a time of major change. The DfES's Future Role of Government Offices (FROGO) programme will have also have significant impact on the children's sector as it proposes to integrate significantly smaller, more 'strategic' teams responsible for the children's sector into Government Offices (GOs). PCS' prognosis is that this will lead to a further reduction in regional operational capacity, possibly to the extent that the CYPFD GO/regional presence is reduced to small numbers of 'change agents' who will only engage local authorities and other organisations at a 'strategic' level. Withdrawing from regional delivery does not appear to sit with the Department's stated position of promoting change locally within the sector"[152].

196. We appreciate PCSU's concerns about operational capacity at regional level. We would also wish to add that, while in principle, devolving control and responsibility to local authorities is welcome, the fact that Local authorities have been largely absolved of their planning and funding responsibilities for schools (in effect giving them less leverage) makes this in practice highly problematic. This is particularly the case in respect of *Every Child Matters,* which envisages a central role for schools.

197. **We are not convinced that the rollout of *Every Child Matters* will be successfully implemented in the context of significant job cuts and restructuring at the DfES and the Children, Young People and Families Directorate in particular. While we appreciate that a more 'strategic' department (and directorate) potentially frees up money for front line services, we are not convinced that this can be achieved at the same time as a major programme of change. Clarification on the kinds of modelling and analysis which have been carried out to demonstrate that the two agendas are complementary is required.**

---

151 EVCM 75

152 EVCM 75

Intra-departmental policy

198. In this and other inquiries, we have been keen to explore the coherence of policy in terms of its fundamental aims, and the implications of coherence (or a lack thereof) for service providers, and ultimately for the people they serve. In section six above, we explored the likely impact of some existing policy tensions on the ability of all schools to play a full and willing part in the *Every Child Matters* programme of reform. Specifically, we asked whether policies promoting increasing independence for schools were compatible with *Every Child Matters*. With regard to standards, the Minister told us that "the inclusion agenda and the standards agenda are two sides of the same coin, and schools understand that"[153]. **We accept that there is a fundamental convergence between the standards and the inclusion agendas. However, what concerns us is that the drivers in the system—including inspection and 'league tables', to give two examples—may not be sufficiently strong to encourage schools to see the two agendas as complementary.**

199. With regard to the independence agenda advanced in the *Five Year Strategy for Children and Learners*[154], and its compatibility with *Every Child Matters*, we are less convinced that there is convergence between the two agendas. As TEN pointed out:

> "The emphasis in the *Five Year Strategy* is strongly on the autonomy of schools—including encouragement to adopt foundation status and acquire foundation bodies with the power to appoint a majority of governors—with an implied diminution in the role of local authorities; in *Every Child Matters*, it is on an area-wide organisation of a range of services through partnership arrangements, the success of which will depend on the role of the local authority and the successful engagement of schools."[155]

This is likely to create fundamental problems in terms of implementing *Every Child Matters*—especially, as discussed in section six above, in the absence of effective policy levers which would address these tensions.

Inter-departmental policy

200. We have also been interested in the course of our inquiry in exploring issues of coherence at the inter-departmental level. *Every Child Matters* creates for the first time a Ministerial position dedicated solely to Children, Young People and Families. The Minister is also part of a cross-governmental Ministerial board with representation from each department. This is a very welcome step forward, and our evidence suggests that this is seen as an almost wholly positive development by all those who have expressed a view on this issue.

201. We do not underestimate the challenges that the Minister faces in pushing children's issues to the top of priority lists in departments which have traditionally been concerned with other priorities. Our experience is that cross-departmental policies – those requiring commitment and co-ordination from different departments—are often the most difficult

153 Q 487

154 ibid

155 EVCM 17, para 3.7.

to deliver. In oral evidence, both the Minister and officials sought to reassure us that they were working hard with colleagues in other departments to secure both a high profile for *Every Child Matters* and a convergence on policies affecting children.

202. We have been particularly interested in establishing during the course of our inquiry how successful the Minister has been to date at securing a high profile for children's services in the Department for Health. We feared that the lack of identified funding to implement the *National Service Framework for Children, Young People and Maternity Services*[156] was indicative of a failure to place children's issues as high on the priority list as other issues. When we put this to the Minister she told us:

> "Yes, there are tensions between the pressures to invest in the acute sector to meet the Health Service performance targets and our desire to expand community children-based services, which on the whole tend to be around the public health agenda. That is why we have these three very important documents—the NSF for Children, the Public Health Service White Paper, and the Chief Nursing Officer's review. That is why we are working with those to try to ensure that appropriate priority decisions are taken at the PCT level to get us the investment we need in children's services. The Health Service has been generously funded over time. It is expanding massively. We need to ensure that some of that expansion comes into children's services. But it is not an easy road—I accept that"[157]

203. Witnesses also told us that they are concerned about tensions in policies pursued by different departments. Youth justice—currently the responsibility of the Home Office—is perceived by many as a particularly problematic area. *Change for Children* explains the relationship between the youth justice and Every Child Matters agenda as follows:

> "Where young people get into trouble with the law, the youth justice system operates alongside the mainstream services. Its main purpose is to reduce offending and it focuses on the factors which underlie offending behaviour. Substance misuse is a particular issue in relation to youth offending as well as truancy, exclusion from school and family problems."[158]

204. However, there is a perception that at a fundamental level, policy aims relating to children have not yet been sufficiently reconciled. The Children's Society argued:

> "If every child really does matter, public and professional confidence in the child protection system must mean that we allow no identifiable holes in the safety net to go unaddressed. The youth justice system represents to us not an accidental hole, but a deliberate tear in the safety net for children and young people. The only way to address the structural and cultural barriers to effective protection in the youth justice system is to undertake a fundamental review of the way in which we treat children in trouble with the law—in our response to Youth Justice: the next steps, we provide more detail of our recommendations"[159]

---

156   ibid

157   q 598

158   ibid, p 16.

159   EVCM 44, para 3.4.3.

The Association of Chief Police Officers made a similar criticism of 'joined-up' policy in relation to youth justice:

"We think it was an error to publish a separate agenda for young people who offend alongside *Every Child Matters* and we think the need to integrate and be very explicit and forward thinking from central Government in the integration of the youth crime agenda with the children's agenda in a way which does not deflect from the obvious priorities around tackling and preventing youth crime, but recognises that children who commit offences, without excusing them or trying to defend them, are exactly the same constituency as children who get excluded from school, children who become in need of protection or have CAMS [Child and Adolescent Mental Health Services] needs, and I think we need to make sure that we do not rehearse that separation in further working around this agenda. It has to be fully integrated across the piece."[160]

205. **We do not think that the challenges involved in dealing with children and young people in custody have been properly addressed by the *Every Child Matters* reforms. The youth justice system is not sufficiently distinct from the adult criminal justice system and is too separate from the mainstream children's legislation and services.**

206. A parallel case has been made with relation to the convergence of policies on asylum and immigration with those advocated in Every Child Matters. Like GPs, schools and others, a statutory duty to co-operate was not placed on the National Asylum Support Service through the Children Act 2004 (although it has since been made clear that immigration services will be encouraged to participate in local partnerships where appropriate). We have received submissions from agencies concerned with the welfare of refugee and asylum-seeking children and families, to suggest that in practice this is likely to militate against the implementation of a system where *every* child really does matter equally. The Refugee Children's Consortium have argued, for example, that the detention of asylum-seeking children in custody is highly problematic and fundamentally in contravention with the expressed aims of Every Child Matters.

207. We asked the Minister to respond to the suggestion that immigration policy was fundamentally in contravention of some of the express aims of *Every Child Matters*. She told us:

"when we considered this issue in relation to the Children Act, we had to be absolutely clear that the primacy in this issue has to be the immigration control and immigration policy. If we had given, for example, the duty to co-operate and duty to safeguard to the Immigration Service, I think that we would have opened a loophole which would have enabled asylum-seeking families and unaccompanied asylum-seeking children to use those particular duties to override the immigration controls and the asylum-seeking controls. That is a difficulty and we had to face up to it. I think that we took the right route, which is that the primacy is on maintaining a fair and just immigration system but, within that, we have always to have regard to the well-being and safety of children—and we do"[161].

---

160 Q 193

161 Q 534

208. We heard evidence that in some cases children's outcomes are secondary to immigration outcomes. We accept that there are sincere attempts to look after children's welfare within the immigration system, but we are concerned that some of the fundamental policy decisions—such as detention of asylum-seeking children - may make the achievement of the five outcomes for these children much more difficult.

Appendix A

Outcomes and Associated Aims

1. Be healthy

Physically healthy

Mentally and emotionally healthy

Sexually healthy

Healthy lifestyles

Choose not to take illegal drugs

Parents, carers and families promote healthy choices

2. Stay safe

Safe from maltreatment, neglect, violence and sexual exploitation

Safe from accidental injury and death

Safe from bullying and discrimination

Safe from crime and anti-social behaviour in and out of school

Have security, stability and are cared for

Parents, carers and families provide safe homes and stability

3. Enjoy and achieve

Ready for school

Attend and enjoy school

Achieve stretching national educational standards at primary school

Achieve personal and social development and enjoy recreation

Achieve stretching national educational standards at secondary school

Parents, carers and families support learning

4. Make a positive contribution

Engage in decision-making and support the community and environment

Engage in law-abiding and positive behaviour in and out of school

Develop positive relationships and choose not to bully and discriminate

Develop self-confidence and successfully deal with significant life changes and challenges

Develop enterprising behaviour

Parents, carers and families promote positive behaviour

5. Achieve economic well-being

Engage in further education, employment or training on leaving school

Ready for employment

Live in decent homes and sustainable communities

Access to transport and material goods

Live in households free from low income

Parents, carers and families are supported to be economically active

Source: Department for Education and Skills, 2004, *Every Child Matters: Change for Children*, pp9.

Conclusions and recommendations

Overarching issues

1. We understand the drive toward rapid transformational change at policy level and think that this is entirely legitimate given the urgency of protecting children better and promoting their development and well-being. However, a Government committed (rightly) to pursuing evidence-based policy has a difficult balance to strike. It is crucial that significant changes are thoroughly trialled and evaluated before roll-out, especially in cases where doing things badly risks worsening outcomes for vulnerable children and young people. (Paragraph 20)

2. The balance between local determination and action from the centre is likely to remain a critical issue as *Every Child Matters* unfolds. Too much central direction risks alienating those on the ground who know a great deal about local circumstances; too little, on the other hand, risks inconsistency and the appearance of gaps in services. In respect of certain aspects of the reforms, our evidence suggests that more central responsibility and direction may be needed than is currently the case. (Paragraph 23)

Involving children, young people and parents

3. We are concerned that significant changes are being made to the Sure Start programme when evidence about the effectiveness of the current system is only just beginning to emerge. This relates back to our wider point about the inherent difficulties of pursuing transformative and rapid change while at the same time maintaining a commitment to evidence-based policy. (Paragraph 39)

Children's Commissioner for England

4. We have yet to be convinced that a Children's Commissioner role primarily defined in terms of promoting children's views, will be as effective in practice as one focused on promoting and protecting children's rights in accordance with the United Nations Convention on the Rights of the Child. (Paragraph 46)

5. We are concerned that the definition of the role of the Children's Commissioner for England as one primarily framed in terms of promoting children's views and concerns, rather than promoting and safeguarding rights, may directly and negatively affect the ability of the Commissioner to achieve improved outcomes for children and young people. (Paragraph 48)

6. We welcome the Minister's assurance that the circumstances in which the Secretary of State will direct the Commissioner will be limited to very serious or tragic cases that require a national inquiry. We also welcome the assurance that the Secretary of State will under no circumstances prevent an inquiry being conducted. However, further clarification of the limits of directive powers should be made through regulation if necessary. Moreover, if there is no intention to ever prevent the Commissioner from conducting a particular inquiry, we fail to see the purpose of a

duty to consult prior to launching an investigation. It is conceivable that future Secretaries of State may not take the same view, and we believe the Government should consider modifying this part of the Act. (Paragraph 52)

7. It should be made clear at the earliest possible opportunity what level of funding will be available for the operation of the Commissioner's office and whether additional resources will be provided if the Secretary of State instructs the Commissioner to conduct a major inquiry which is likely to tie up large amounts of resources and personnel time—or whether it is expected that those costs will be met out of current allocations. (Paragraph 53)

8. We are reassured to hear the Minister's assessment of her likely working relationship with the Children's Commissioner for England as one that was likely to be uncomfortable at times—in our view, anything less would be profoundly worrying, and as a Committee, we will look for evidence that the relationship between the Children's Commissioner and Ministers is developing in an appropriate way. (Paragraph 54)

9. We are pleased that the three existing Commissioners are committed to working with the Commissioner for England to resolve any problems concerning jurisdiction. Their suggestion that a memorandum of understanding should be drawn up at the earliest possible convenience seems a productive way forward, and is one possible way to broach issues of jurisdiction. This would also provide an opportunity to capitalise on the valuable experience of the three existing Commissioners—which they are extremely keen to share with the appointee for England. (Paragraph 57)

10. We suggest that a fully independent review of the role and remit of the Children's Commissioner for England should be commissioned within three years of appointment. This should include analysis of the effectiveness of the Commissioner post, with particular reference to the impact of the statutory framework. Amendments to statute should be pursued if the review indicates that the Children's Commissioner is unduly constrained by the existing legal framework. (Paragraph 59)

11. To preserve independence of the Children's Commissioner for England, there needs to be a strong link between the Commissioner and Parliament. By custom and practice Her Majesty's Chief Inspector of Schools reports directly to Parliament through this Committee and we envisage a similar relationship with the Children's Commissioner for England. (Paragraph 60)

Integrated services at the frontline

12. The DfES told us that they would shortly launch a prospectus on Extended Schools. Where conversion to an Extended School is being considered, we recommend that the prospectus should stress the benefits of planning with local partners, including voluntary services, who often have wide experience of engaging vulnerable groups, to ensure local needs are met. (Paragraph 72)

Workforce development and training needs

13. A toolkit on multi-agency working is scheduled to be released in April 2005—and we will be interested to see what prominence is given to challenges around the reconfiguring of professional identities and responsibilities that working in a multi-agency team is likely to present. (Paragraph 78)

14. The introduction of an integrated inspection framework offers a further opportunity to emphasise the importance of integrated working at the front line, and we hope the final guidance on integrated inspection later this year will focus in part on this issue. (Paragraph 82)

15. We are not convinced that workforce training needs for all in-service staff are likely to be given the priority across the board at the local level that they merit and which the Government anticipates. While we appreciate that there are significant resources already invested in the training of children's professionals in some sectors, we are particularly concerned about the priority which will be attached to *Every Child Matters*-related workforce development for staff in other sectors, and particularly the health services. (Paragraph 89)

16. Department of Health officials told us that there was no ring-fenced money at departmental level for training . With little or no extra resources identified for the implementation of *Every Child Matters* in general, we are concerned that with many pressures on primary care trusts and other budgets, crucial *Every Child Matters*-related training will not be given the priority it deserves. (Paragraph 90)

17. We would urge that the presumption against an entitlement to training—with a pooled fund at interdepartmental level to support it—is reconsidered. Such a move would send out clear signals to local areas that training and workforce development were being given a high priority, and would also provide vital initial resources to address some of the staff development and training needs arising from the implementation of the *Every Child Matters* agenda. (Paragraph 92)

Child indexes

18. In the past, this committee has been concerned that crucial policy decisions are sometimes taken without sufficient research or evaluation of existing practice. In this case, the fundamental decision to go ahead with child indexes appears to have been taken before the activities of the Information Sharing and Assessment Trailblazers could be fully analysed. (Paragraph 112)

19. We are not convinced that sufficient evidence currently exists to justify the commissioning of the proposed IT-based child indexes. We have significant reservations about whether this will represent the best use of resources and very significant concerns about critical issues such as security, confidentiality and access arrangements. We are concerned in particular that the current research evidence does not conclusively demonstrate that expenditure in this area is the best way of improving outcomes for children. (Paragraph 113)

20. We welcome the news that further evaluative work on the impact of indexes in Trailblazer areas is now being planned, and that the results of this will be used to inform the business case for implementation. This research should analyse the comparative benefit of the indexes as a means of improving outcomes and other ways of improving information-sharing within and between professionals. (Paragraph 114)

Common Assessment Framework

21. It is essential that the design and implementation of the Common Assessment Framework takes place at a pace that allows informed development. The commitment to further testing and assessment before national rollout is therefore extremely welcome. While it is sensible that the assessments will examine the impacts of Common Assessment Framework on services, we would also hope that they take a broader view and examine the extent to which the Common Assessment Framework is leading to improved outcomes for children, young people and families. (Paragraph 126)

Pacing change

22. The Government has made a welcome commitment to respecting local needs, and putting control over change in local hands and we would encourage them to maintain this commitment. Statutory guidance should contain explicit reference to the need to protect front line services during transition, and to implement change at a pace suited to local needs. At the national level the Government can assist by remaining alert for any evidence that unintended negative side-effects of change are occurring, and, especially, that any decrease in the effectiveness of critical front line and child protection services is taking place. (Paragraph 131)

Integrated inspection

23. We maintain that for inspection to serve as a lever for improvement, there needs to be a clear process linking inspection findings, communication of these findings to service(s) inspected, and suitable intervention to bring about change. (Paragraph 140)

24. To play the critical role in *Every Child Matters* that the Government envisages, integrated inspection must ultimately contribute to the improvement of services. We would welcome clarification on how this will happen with regard to inspections of children's services. The specific procedures which will be triggered should a local area be deemed by integrated inspection to be failing require clearer explanation. In particular, it needs to be made clear how the findings of area reviews will be played back to individual service providers, and how these will be used to bring about improvement. (Paragraph 143)

25. We are not convinced that the levers for participation suggested by the Government will provide the necessary safeguards. This is especially true in the light of policy tensions in the DfES, which appear to be producing contradictory drivers and to be

demanding conflicting responses from schools and service providers. (Paragraph 150)

26. We await final confirmation of the details of integrated inspection, but we are deeply concerned that some schools, GPs and other services not under a statutory duty to collaborate in Children's Trust agreements may choose, for one reason or another, not to participate. This has the potential to fundamentally undermine the aims and intentions of *Every Child Matters*. It is unlikely that the current incentives and penalties in the system will be adequate to make reluctant schools, in particular, co-operate. The Government needs to clarify what additional incentives will be introduced into the system to address this issue, and especially, what changes will be made to the framework for the inspection of schools. (Paragraph 162)

27. Statutory guidance and other communications which concern themselves with budget-pooling need to make absolutely clear that local areas should not pursue such pooling for its own sake. Until sufficient evidence has been amassed from Pathfinder Children's Trusts on best practice in this area, it would be preferable to give a clear steer for local areas to thoroughly analyse the benefits likely to accrue from budget-pooling before embarking on the process. (Paragraph 169)

Director of Children's Services

28. The DfES is currently consulting on the Director of Children's Services role. When statutory guidance is finally issued, it must make explicit the actions which will be open to Directors of Children's Services should essential partners fail to co-operate. (Paragraph 176)

Funding: overall costs of reform

29. We think—and our concern is amplified by what witnesses have told us—that the additional resources needed to 'bridge' the transition from 'fire fighting' to more effective preventive, universally accessible services are unlikely to be found through 'efficiency savings' generated by services working in a more 'joined-up' way. (Paragraph 186)

30. The evidence we have seen has not convinced us that the financial implications of the *Every Child Matters* programme of reform have been properly assessed or comprehensively modelled, and it is therefore not clear on what basis the Government is able to assume that *Every Child Matters* will be largely self-financing. We recognise and welcome the significant extra resources for primary school capital projects, announced in Budget 2005 which, it is intended, will be used partly to support the *Every Child Matters* agenda. However, we are still unclear as to whether capital building, adaptation or maintenance costs associated with the roll-out of Extended Schools and Sure Start Children's Centres have been properly modelled. (Paragraph 188)

31. We are doubtful that a policy as ambitious as *Every Child Matters* can be funded in the main from existing budgets. Better deployment of existing resources is a laudable aim, but we believe the Government needs to lead from the top on this issue and

build up an evidence base which demonstrates how this can be achieved in practice. (Paragraph 189)

32. Our evidence demonstrates that at the very least, in respect of some specific areas of policy there is a strong case for identifying additional funds for implementation, over and above those which have already been put aside. These areas include, but are not limited to, workforce development and the setup and maintenance of Children's Trusts. The Government should therefore consider committing additional dedicated resources—cross-departmentally and ring-fenced if appropriate—to enable successful implementation of *Every Child Matters*. (Paragraph 190)

DfES restructuring

33. We are not convinced that the rollout of *Every Child Matters* will be successfully implemented in the context of significant job cuts and restructuring at the DfES and the Children, Young People and Families Directorate in particular. While we appreciate that a more 'strategic' department (and directorate) potentially frees up money for front line services, we are not convinced that this can be achieved at the same time as a major programme of change. Clarification on the kinds of modelling and analysis which have been carried out to demonstrate that the two agendas are complementary is required. (Paragraph 197)

Intra-departmental policy

34. We accept that there is a fundamental convergence between the standards and the inclusion agendas. However, what concerns us is that the drivers in the system – including inspection and 'league tables', to give two examples—may not be sufficiently strong to encourage schools to see the two agendas as complementary. (Paragraph 198)

Interdepartmental policy

35. We do not think that the challenges involved in dealing with children and young people in custody have been properly addressed by the *Every Child Matters* reforms. The youth justice system is not sufficiently distinct from the adult criminal justice system and is too separate from the mainstream children's legislation and services. (Paragraph 205)

36. We heard evidence that in some cases children's outcomes are secondary to immigration outcomes. We accept that there are sincere attempts to look after children's welfare within the immigration system, but we are concerned that some of the fundamental policy decisions – such as detention of asylum-seeking children - may make the achievement of the five outcomes for these children much more difficult. (Paragraph 208).

Formal minutes

Wednesday 23 March 2005

Members present:
Mr Barry Sheerman, in the Chair

David Chaytor	Helen Jones
Valerie Davey	Mr Kerry Pollard
Jeff Ennis	Jonathan Shaw
Mr John Greenway	

The Committee deliberated.

Draft Report (Every Child Matters), proposed by the Chairman, brought up and read.

Ordered, That the Chairman's draft Report be read a second time, paragraph by paragraph.

Paragraphs 1 to 208 read and agreed to.

Summary agreed to.

Resolved, That the Report be the Ninth Report of the Committee to the House.

Ordered, That the Chairman do make the Report to the House.

Ordered, That the provisions of Standing Order No. 134 (Select committees (reports)) be applied to the Report.

Several papers were ordered to be appended to the Minutes of Evidence.

Ordered, That the Appendices to the Minutes of Evidence taken before the Committee be reported to the House.

Several Memoranda were ordered to be reported to the House.

The Committee further deliberated.

[Adjourned to a day and time to be fixed by the Chairman

Witnesses

Monday 29 November 2004

Lord Laming of Tewin, Chairman, Victoria Climbié
Mr Philip Collins, Director, Social Market Foundation

Monday 13 December 2004

Mr David Bell, Her Majesty's Chief Inspector of Schools, Ofsted, **Mrs Anna Walker CB**, Chief Executive, Healthcare Commission, **Mr Steve Bundred**, Chief Executive, Audit Commission and **Mr David Behan**, Chief Inspector, Commission for Social Care Inspection.

Monday 20 December 2004

Dame Gill Morgan, Chief Executive, NHS Confederation, **Mr John Coughlan**, Co-Chair, Children and Families Committee, Association of Directors of Social Services, **Cllr James Kempton**, Vice-Chair, Children and Young People's Board, Local Government Association, **Mr David Hawker**, Incoming Chair, Association of Directors of Education and Children's Services and **Chief Constable Terry Grange**, Lead on Child Protection, Association of Chief Police Officers

Monday 10 January 2005

Mr Peter Newell, Children's Rights Alliance for England and Adviser, European Network of Ombudspeople for Children, and **Ms Mary Marsh**, Chief Executive, NSPCC.
Mr Nigel Williams, Commissioner for Children and Young People for Northern Ireland, **Mr Peter Clarke**, Children's Commissioner for Wales and **Professor Kathleen Marshall**, Commissioner for Children and Young People for Scotland

Monday 24 January 2005

Ms Bridget Lindley, Deputy Chief Executive, Family Rights Group, Family Welfare Association and Parentline Plus, representing the Family Policy Alliance, and **Dr Deborah Ghate**, Director, Policy Research Bureau.
Professor Hedy Cleaver, Professorial Research Fellow, Royal Holloway, University of London, **Mr Richard Thomas**, Information Commissioner and **Dr Eileen Munro**, Reader in Social Policy, London School of Economics.

Wednesday 2 February 2005

Mr Tom Jeffery, Director-General, **Ms Anne Jackson**, Director, Strategy Group, **Ms Sheila Scales**, Director, Local Transformation Group, **Ms Althea, Efunshile**, Director, Safeguarding Young Children Group, **Dr Jeannette Pugh**, Director, Children's Workforce Unit, Children, Young People and Families Directorate, Department for Education and Skills, and **Mr Mark Davies**, Deputy Director of Care Services, Children and Mental Health, Department of Health.

Wednesday 9 February 2005

Rt Hon Margaret Hodge MBE MP, Minister for Children, Young People and Families

List of written evidence

1	The Information Commissioner	EVCM 4
2	Royal College of Nursing	EVCM 5
3	Contact a Family	EVCM 8
4	National Youth Agency	EVCM 12
5	Association of Directors of Education and Children's Services and the Confederation of Education Service Managers	EVCM 15
6	Professor Peter Moss	EVCM 16
7	Education Network, Democratic Health Network	EVCM 17
8	YMCA	EVCM 20
9	Royal College of General Practitioners	EVCM 22
10	Association of Teachers and Lectures (ATL)	EVCM 23
11	National Union of Teachers	EVCM 24
12	The Foyer Federation	EVCM 29
13	Centrepoint	EVCM 30
14	General Teaching Council	EVCM 31
15	National Society for the Prevention of Cruelty to Children (NSPCC)	EVCM 32
16	Woman's Aid Federation of England	EVCM 34
17	Refugee Children's Consortium	EVCM 38
18	Northgate Information Solutions	EVCM 40
19	National Association of Head Teachers (NAHT)	EVCM 42
20	The Children's Society	EVCM 44
21	Barnardo's	EVCM 45
22	Refugee Council	EVCM 47
23	Family Policy Alliance	EVCM 48
24	Audit Commission	EVCM 49
25	LGA	EVCM 51
26	4Children	EVCM 54
27	Association of Directors of Social Services	EVCM 57
28	DfES	EVCM 58
29	Commission for Social Care Inspection	EVCM 60
30	Association of Chief Police Officers	EVCM 62
31	Peter Newell	EVCM 63
32	Children's Commissioners	EVCM 64
33	Healthcare Commission	EVCM 65
34	Information Commissioner	EVCM 66
35	Eileen Munro	EVCM 67
36	Policy Research Bureau	EVCM 68
37	Family Policy Alliance	EVCM 69
38	Professor Hedy Cleaver	EVCM 72
39	NSPCC	EVCM 73
40	Margaret Hodge MP	EVCM 74
41	PCS	EVCM 75

List of unprinted written evidence

Additional papers have been received from the following and have been reported to the House but to save printing costs they have not been printed and copies have been placed in the House of Commons library where they may be inspected by members. Other copies are in the Record Office, House of Lords and are available to the public for inspection. Requests for inspection should be addressed to the Record Office, House of Lords, London SW1. (Tel 020 7219 3074) hours of inspection are from 9:30am to 5:00pm on Mondays to Fridays.

EVCM 01 Skill: National Bureau for Students with Disabilities

EVCM 02 Community Play Rangers in Bath and North East Somerset

EVCM 03 National Association of Educational Inspectors Advisors and Consultants

EVCM 06 British Medical Association

EVCM 07 The Oakfield Crew

EVCM 09 Parentkind

EVCM 10 Skills for Health

EVCM 11 National Association of Connexions Partnerships (NACP)

EVCM 13 Independent Children's Homes Association

EVCM 14 SkillsActive

EVCM 15 Association of Directors of Education and Children's Services and the Confederation of Education Service Managers

EVCM 18 Children's Play Council

EVCM 19 CCPR

EVCM 21 ISCG

EVCM 25 Family Planning Association (FPA)

EVCM 26 School Home Support

EVCM 27 Association of London Chief Education Officers (ALCEO)

EVCM 28 National Day Nurseries Association (NDNA)

EVCM 33 Mayor of London

EVCM 35 Campaign for Learning

EVCM 36 National College for School Leadership

EVCM 37 Association of Colleges (AoC)

EVCM 39 Evan Reynolds

EVCM 41 United Nations High Commissioner for Refugees (UNHCR)

EVCM 43 Disability Rights Commission

EVCM 50 from the NASUWT;

EVCM 53 from the National College for School Leadership;

EVCM 55 from NIACE

EVCM 56 from the National Childminding Association

EVCM 59 AoC

EVCM 71 CHANT

Reports from the Education and Skills Committee, Session 2004–05

First Report	Public Expenditure on Education and Skills	HC 168
Second Report	Education Outside the Classroom	HC 120
Third Report	UK e-University	HC 205
Fourth Report	The Work of the Committee in 2004	HC 359
Fifth Report	Secondary Education	HC 86
Sixth Report	National Skills Strategy: 14–19 Education	HC 37
Seventh Report	Prison Education	HC 114
First Special Report	Government Response to the Committee's Fifth Report of Session 2003-04: Secondary Education: Teacher Retention	HC 85
Second Special Report	Government's and Ofsted's Response to the Committee's Sixth Report of Session 2003–04: The Work of Ofsted	HC 206

Printed in the United Kingdom by The Stationery Office Limited
4/2005   304474   19585

ISBN 0-215-02389-7

9 780215 023896